Birdhouse Builder's Manual

By
Charles Grodski and Roger Schroeder

Measured Drawings by
Wayne Pimental

FOX BOOKS
Fox Chapel Publishing Co Inc.

Publisher: Alan Giagnocavo
Project Editor: Ayleen Stellhorn
Desktop Specialist: Linda L. Eberly, Eberly Designs Inc.
Interior Photography: Roger Schroeder
Cover Photography: Roger Schroeder, Robert Polett

ISBN # 1-56523-100–7

To order your copy of this book,
please send check or money order
for $19.95 plus $2.50 shipping to:
Fox Book Orders
1970 Broad Street
East Petersburg, PA 17520

Manufactured in Korea

DEDICATION

To our wives Polly and Sheila, and to our family and friends for their continued love and support

TABLE OF CONTENTS

Chuck Grodski

Chuck Grodski is a nationally recognized designer and builder of birdhouses. A native of Long Island, New York, Chuck went from being a farm boy to a machinist for Grumman Aerospace, a carpenter and a buyer for antique dealers. He estimates that he has built over 1,000 birdhouses that have found yards as far away as California.

Chuck lives with his wife Polly in St. James, Long Island, New York.

Roger Schroeder

Roger Schroeder's success as a writer began when he stopped trying to write the great American novel. Instead, he turned to writing about his hobby: woodworking. Sharpening his skills and his photography and expanding his interests, he went on to author 15 books and over 200 magazine articles. Ranging in scope from woodcarving to housebuilding to scrimshaw, the books include such titles as *How to Carve Wildfowl, Timber Frame Construction, Carving Signs,* and *Making Toys.* Despite the prolific output, this has not been Roger's full-time profession. He is a high school English teacher, specializing in teaching writing and research.

When Roger is not teaching, he is lecturing on how to make wood into furniture, houses and sculpture. In the remaining time he is an amateur cabinetmaker—specializing in Victorian reproductions—and an amateur bird carver who has received a number of blue ribbons for his natural wood sculptures.

Roger lives with his wife Sheila in Amityville, Long Island, New York.

My wife, Sheila, and I nearly missed Chuck Grodski's property as we drove along on one of Long Island, New York's most scenic roads. She had caught sight of an

A large sign introduces visitors to Chuck Grodski's home and workshop.

elaborate Victorian-style birdhouse behind a high hedge near the road. On a bracket was a sign reading "Custom Birdhouses." After making a U-turn, we pulled into Chuck's yard, encouraged by a welcome sign. What we discovered was a heaven for birds.

Chuck has over 60 birdhouses on his property. Some are simple, yet colorful boxes. Others have elaborate ornamentation. A few are made with stones for façade and chimney. All are extremely imaginative and creative.

Chuck's passion for birdhouses began with an insect problem. He found it annoying to sit outdoors on the expansive deck he

had built and have to swat away the bugs. Having been born and raised in what was once a rural tract of America, he decided to encourage birds to nest on his property to cut down on the insect population. The more birdhouses he built, the more the insects disappeared.

Word spread, as is always the case when dealing with the talented, that a man in the neighborhood was designing and constructing unique birdhouses. People came by asking for his work and Chuck has been busy ever since.

Today, visitors like myself and my wife take note of the elaborate birdhouses near the road and stop in for a walk around the property. Not everyone makes a purchase, but each person leaves with good feelings about Chuck's special talents.

Having been a writer in the woodworking field for nearly 20 years, I quickly saw the possibility of collaborating on a book about Chuck's work. We decided on a step-by-step book that would show the reader how to build four very different birdhouses. *The Birdhouse Builder's Manual* is the result.

Some of his impressive birdhouses can be easily seen from the busy road that passes his property.

The first project is a simple one with a twin-gable roof. The birdhouse contains two compartments for nesting. With a pair of chimneys added for interest, the house can be painted in a variety of pleasing colors that should delight birds and owners alike.

The second project is a log cabin, also with two compartments. What makes this a charming addition to a backyard is the chimney constructed of beach stones. An overhang and posts in the front of the house create the look of a porch.

A pair of wagon wheels with three long

Working in a simple basement shop, Chuck crafts a wide variety of birdhouses.

houses attached between the wheels is the third project. Each house has three compartments. And each wheel is cleverly constructed of butted-together pieces of curved wood.

The fourth project is one of Chuck's masterpieces of design. Inspired by Victorian homes, the house gives birds access through the many dormers and doors. Columns, ready-made moldings and finials also adorn this three-foot-long birdhouse. Richly colored to look like a Victorian painted lady, the house could not be called complete until Chuck topped it with a tower and a working bell.

Each of the projects comprises step-by-

step photos. You will see Chuck in action as he starts with a few pieces of wood in the basement shop where he works so efficiently. There, on a paint-spattered workbench, he fashions some of the finest birdhouses you may ever see.

Before you go out to purchase wood at the local lumber yard or home center, read the section entitled "Getting Started." Learn which tools, what species of wood and which adhesives and paints work best for Chuck. You may already have enough materials in your basement or garage to build a simple house in one or two weekends.

In the gallery section, you will see the products of Chuck's genius: churches, stone

His birdhouses range from simple, unpainted boxes to the elaborate.

houses, temples and mansions. There are fanciful birdhouses as well. On a maple tree near his home is a partial golf bag made of wood. The wings from a furniture griffin adorn the "bag" that is filled with cut-down clubs. The rim is trimmed with painted golf balls. He calls the piece, complete with a perch fashioned from a putter, *Winged Victory*. A discarded bowling pin became a home for birds when he cut it in half, hollowed it and rejoined the pieces. Another creation, *The All-Seeing Eye,* came about after he started putting pieces of wood together without a fixed idea of where he was going. When he took off his glasses to wipe away sawdust, he decided in Eureka! fashion to build an eye by having wood fanning out from a circle.

People ask Chuck where he gets his ideas. He says simply, "The inspiration comes from the man up there," and tilts his head heavenward.

There is some earthbound help as well. He quickly gives credit to his daughter, Marie, for putting some finishing touches on either the houses or the posts they perch on. Possessing an

Chuck's daughter, Marie Todaro, helps with the painting.

artist's eye, she adds delicately painted flowers, leaves and vines where they will be the most attractive.

It was both educational and inspirational for me to have spent a few weeks in the summer of 1997 to watch Chuck work. Each day I longed to return home and build my own birdhouses. Finally, by the end of that summer, I had designed two projects: one based on a Rhode Island stone-ender built by my friend and wood sculptor Armand LaMontagne; the other a Craftsman-style house. Both show off the best of natural wood and stone. Completed, they are featured on page 12.

Happy birdhouse building!

Roger Schroeder
Amityville, New York

This Adirondack-style mountain lodge has a stone façade, asphalt shingles and eight holes.

Described as having a Disneyland look, this house sports spires and minarets. It was mounted on a table base.

This fiberglass bust sits atop a birdhouse column.

The manor house with dormers and cupola has 40 columns.

The martin house has 16 holes, eight on each side. Birds love the grapevines for perching.

The twin-gable house, with two separate compartments, is given the look of worn paint. It is a good seller.

Sometimes the colors chosen are based on the paint cans closest to the work station.

The house has a chalet look. It is easily mounted on a tree or post.

This shade of purple is a favorite with customers.

Notice the details around the windows. The post with its Victorian brackets enhances the look of the station.

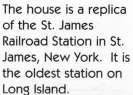

The house is a replica of the St. James Railroad Station in St. James, New York. It is the oldest station on Long Island.

Whimsical, this house incorporates stars into the design.

Many customers find this a cute house. The brackets under the roof give it added style.

Titled *The All-Seeing Eye,* the house is made from plywood.

The house has a carnival look with patriotic colors.

Based on the World's Fair of 1939, The Trylon tower and Perisphere are unique birdhouse constructions.

GALLERY

Some people confuse this house with the Leaning Tower of Pisa. It is a graduated octagon about six feet tall.

A roughsawn house will weather well. The red will eventually turn a rust color.

This is a smaller version of the St. James Railroad Station. The trestle complements the building.

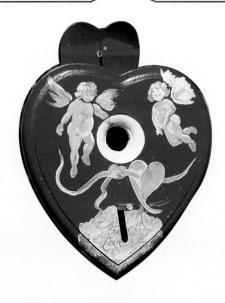

This is a plywood birdhouse. People find the patriotic colors appealing.

Perfect for a Valentine's Day gift, the house was painted by Marie Todaro. A house like this one is suitable as indoor decor.

A fun piece, this house receives lots of compliments.

The house has obvious appeal to golfers. The perch is a putter and the wings were taken from a discarded piece of furniture. Most people comment on the perch.

This birdhouse is replica of an Episcopal church in St. James, Long Island, New York.

Victorian colors make this a popular birdhouse.

This house is a "Russian-style tragedy." The turnings were purchased at lumber yards and home centers.

The Victorian-style house has 12 compartments. It is a best seller.

Based on a Massachusetts church, this birdhouse is over five feet tall.

What gives this Victorian-style house interest are the turnings.

The Victorian-inspired house has received national recognition.

This is an ambitious house with over 400 hours invested in it.

This is a Victorian-style farmhouse.

The octagon steeple makes this a popular birdhouse.

This house is a replica of a Presbyterian church in Smithtown, Long Island, New York.

The house has 12 holes and an asphalt roof.

Inspired by a nearby Presbyterian church on Long Island, New York, the house has 20 holes.

Birdhouses built to look like churches are popular items. The church is unique because the windows, done by Marie Todaro, are painted to look like stained glass.

The pedestal will eventually have two other birdhouses mounted on it. Artist and co-author Chuck Grodski stands beside his creation.

Made from cedar and antlers, this house looks like it belongs in the Northwest.

This Adirondack house was inspired by houses in New York State's Adirondack Mountains region.

Based on a Rhode Island stone-ender built by wood sculptor Armand LaMontagne, the house is made of redwood with cedar shingles. It was built by co-author Roger Schroeder.

Most people buy this house as an interior decoration.

Based on a Craftsman-style house, this cedar and redwood birdhouse has six compartments. It was built by co-author Roger Schroeder.

The log cabin house is made entirely from cedar. The central chimney is made from beach stones.

The chalet-style house is popular because of the various roof lines and colors.

The galleries under each perch add interest.

This is the "Star Spangled Decoration."

Based on Manhattan's Empire State Building, the house is mounted on a hand-painted pedestal.

This many-compartment mansion was inspired by the Taj Mahal.

Inspired by the Greek Parthenon, the columns were made with a router.

This six-hole house has the look of a town hall. On top is a bell tower.

This house is a replica of the Stony Brook Museum, Stony Brook, New York. The fluted post lends an especially attractive touch.

Marie Borella requested a Gothic-style church. She passed away before the birdhouse was completed. It is dedicated to her memory.

A wagon wheel construction, this house has nine holes in three separate houses.

The English Union Jack inspired the one-hole house.

This one-hole house has a lot of detail. It is made from pine with an asphalt roof.

The country look of this house, with its worn paint and vines, is popular.

This birdhouse is a replica of the seventeenth-century house behind it.

Adjoining birdhouses make for an interesting "urban" design.

Designed to look like a saltbox, this is an easy house to make.

This birdhouse is a simple saltbox with two compartments.

Made from staves, much as a barrel is made, this round house is capped with an octagon roof.

Topping the birdhouse is a replica of an eighteenth century witch's ball, thought to keep witches away!

This is a model of a yet-to-be reno-vated church in Lindenhurst, Long Island, New York. Marie Todaro painted the stained-glass windows.

Because the summer heat tends to build up inside the light-house, it was vented with small louvers.

The tapered octagon lighthouse is 10 feet tall. Painted by Marie Todaro, it has a light that goes on at night.

Supporting a chalet-style house, the post can be described as a see-through design.

The Empire State Building was the model for this four-foot-tall birdhouse.

Customers find two hearts just as appealing as one.

The Victorian farm-house is mounted on a post and painted with complementary colors.

The log cabin has six holes with two chimneys. The roof is made of reproduction eighteenth century clapboard.

The multi-level structure was inspired by a pagoda.

The idea for this fortress came from discarded dentil molding.

Power Tools

We are fortunate to live in the twentieth century with the tool technology available to us. Only a century ago, craftsmen had to rely primarily on hand tools. Hand saws, hand planes and hand drills were necessary and plentiful in a shop. Today, with home and tool centers, we are able to power up our work spaces with a variety of sophisticated tools and speed up our productivity.

Compact and economical benchtop table saws are ideal for birdhouse construction.

The workhorse of nearly every production and home shop is the **table saw.** It can rip the length of a board, crosscut it, put grooves in it and cut fancy joints. Although many manufacturers now have on the market what are known as cabinet and contractor's saws, benchtop saws are available.

Inexpensive and portable, these saws are ideal for small-scale work such as birdhouses, and they can perform the same operations as their larger counterparts.

The **band saw** is another ideal tool for the home craftsperson. Not only can it do some of the operations of the table saw—ripping, crosscutting—it can also cut out intricate patterns and curves. Capable of ripping thick boards into thin ones, band saws also come in benchtop models. There are even three-wheel band saws available that offer the deep throat found on the larger two-wheel saws.

The band saw is a valuable tool for cutting out profiles.

The **drill press** is a power tool than allows you to drill and bore with precision and offers far more accuracy and safety than a power drill. Drill presses are available in floor models as well as benchtop sizes. The smaller drill presses can handle most small projects and are economical.

When it comes to removing wood abrasively, the combination tool of **belt and disc sander** is a must. The tool is as much a shaper as it is a sander, and it is ideal for refining angles and flattening surfaces. As its name suggests, it is really two tools. One is a continuous revolving belt; the other a steel disc with abrasive paper attached. Like the table saw, band saw and drill press, floor models and benchtop machines can be purchased.

For shaping and fast sanding, use a belt and disc sander.

Sometimes referred to as a chop saw, the **miter saw** replaces the table saw for many operations. The word miter means to cut at an angle, and that is what this saw does best. More sophisticated miter saws cut at compound angles, meaning that two angles can be cut at once. Sliding compound miter saws are mounted on rails that allow you to crosscut wide stock. Miter saws come with a variety of blade diameters as large as 12 inches.

Although it is not used as much as other power tools, the **oscillating spindle sander** is finding its way into more home shops. Rubber sanding drums, made for abrasive sleeves, sand curves. Unfortunately, they often burn the wood. The oscillating spindle sander, however, moves the drum up and down, cutting down not only on burn marks but also on wear.   Kits can be purchased to convert the drill press into an oscillating spindle sander.

The **router** is as common as the table saw in nearly all shops. With a variety of cutting bits available, it can tackle nearly any profile as well as remove wood background and cut grooves. In the past decade, the router has undergone a design revolution.

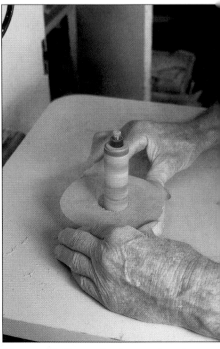

The oscillating spindle sander shapes and sands without burning the wood.

Instead of having to lower a router with its bit rotating at 25,000 revolutions per minute into the middle of a panel, the plunge router allows you to place the tool on the wood, then lower the carriage and bit before cutting. The plunging action makes the machine safer and reduces potential damage to the wood. A router table also allows you to shape small pieces of wood, such as the rounded logs for the log cabin project.

The **air nailer** is not for every shop, but it does make nailing a pleasure. If you plan to go into production work, it is a must. The tool not only drives the nail in with a single pull of a trigger, but it also sets a nail below the surface of the wood, thereby eliminating having to use a nail set. (A compressor with at least 3/4 horsepower is required.)

Portable drills do not replace drill presses, but they can go where no large machine can. What has revolutionized the portable drill is that cords are no longer necessary. Movement is virtually limitless now that battery packs have replaced the cord and extension cord.

All the power tools have a wide variety of accessories that can be purchased. Sanders have a variety of abrasives; table saws have a wide selection of blades; routers have hundreds of possible bits. For birdhouse construction it

An air nailer is worth the expense if you intend to do production work.

will be worthwhile to invest in a selection of tools for boring holes.

Twist drills make holes for nails, screws and bolts. They are sized by the $1/32$ inch and start at $1/16$ inch. **Spade bits** are another accessory worth having. Called spade bits because of their flat shape, they come in large widths and are ideal for drilling large diameter holes. **Hole saws** are a necessity when drilling fairly wide diameter holes. These come with a pilot bit or mandrel and interchangeable round blades. The hole saw, rather than just boring the wood, removes a disc of wood. Hole saws start at $1/2$-inch

Spade bits are a good investment when boring holes.

diameter and range over three inches in diameter.

Measuring and Marking Tools

Nearly everyone is accustomed to seeing or using a **retractable tape measure.** It has a flexible steel tape that measures from as little as three feet to as much as 30 feet in length. It is probably the most versatile measuring tool you can own.

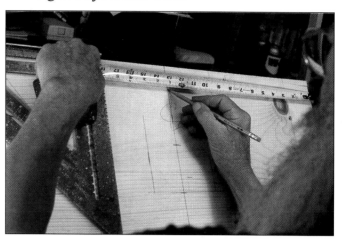

The retractable tape measure is your best measuring tool.

Just as useful is a tool that is not flexible at all: the **bench rule.** Usually made of aluminum, the bench rule can be as short as one foot or as long as five feet. It is ideal for measuring and providing an edge with which to draw straight lines.

A close relative of the bench rule is the **T-square.** Called that because of its shape, a steel T-square anchors itself to the edge of a board and allows you to lay out parallel lines and cut material with-

A steel bench rule measures and provides a straight edge for marking or cutting.

out the edge moving.

The **miter square** performs three functions: it checks the squareness of a board; it is a measuring tool; and it provides an edge to draw a straight line.

Still another straight edge is the **framing square.** This, too, will check the square of wood and offers measurements and an edge for laying out lines.

The rafter square is excellent for laying out 45 degree roof pitches.

A **rafter square** is useful when laying out roof pitches of 45 degrees. The four birdhouses featured in the how-to section have roof pitches of 45 degrees.

A shop is not complete without **clamps.** For years woodworkers used cumbersome steel pipe or bar clamps to hold wood together for gluing or assembly. Today a variety of quick-grip clamps are available ranging in a variety of sizes. For most birdhouses, clamps that span at least two feet should be adequate. They will supply sufficient pressure for assembly and gluing.

Wood

Nearly 100,000 species of wood have been identified in the world. For most birdhouses, you should be concerned with only two: **pine** and **cedar.** You may want to experiment with other woods—and even plywood—but pine and cedar are the two woods that Chuck finds to be the best suited for making durable birdhouses.

There are two types of cedar readily available: white and red. The red cedar is commonly used in pencils. The white cedar is commercially used for shingles and decking. The cedar you purchase at the lumber company is most likely white cedar. Highly decay resistant, it is ideal for birdhouse construction. It can be painted or left natural to eventually turn a silvery gray.

Pine is the most commonly available wood. White pine, sugar pine and yellow pine are all varieties of this wood that have been used for just about everything: houses, furniture and even ships' masts. Pine does have its drawbacks. For one, it is not rot-resistant. Also, it often contains knots which can bleed through paint or even fall out. If bought as clear or knot-free wood, it is very costly. However, knotty pine is inexpensive and, when primed and painted, will guarantee a birdhouse that should last a good ten years. The Victorian mansion was made almost entirely of pine.

Fasteners

Ranging in size from tiny brads to bolts that are several feet in length, fasteners are what hold our world together. For birdhouses, you should have a supply of **galvanized nails** and **stainless steel screws** on hand, even if you own an air nailer. How long should your nails and screws be? The best rule of thumb is to have at least one half the fastener extend into the secondary piece of wood.

Invest in stainless steel screws.

Adhesives

Many adhesives are on the market, from marine epoxies to white glue. Two that you will find useful for the projects in this book are **Titebond® II and PL200®.**

Titebond® II is a good adhesive.

A water-resistant glue, Titebond® II is ideal for outdoor projects, birdhouses included. The glue will hold up to freezing and thawing, but it is not recommended for wood that will be continuously submersed in water. This should not be the case with birdhouses.

PL200® is a construction adhesive. Guaranteed waterproof, it is unaffected by freezing and thawing. Made for paneling, drywall and other light construction, the adhesive is ideal for bonding stones to wood. PL200® was used to hold the stones to the wall of the log cabin project. Be warned, however, that it is extremely flammable, that it is harmful or fatal if swallowed, and that the vapors may cause eye, skin and respiratory irritation.

Paints and Caulking

There are many paint products available to the birdhouse builder, from **primers** to **oil paints** to **latex.** Most of us have used latex to paint a room or exterior siding. It applies easily and dries quickly. It is also easy to clean a latex brush with just soap and water.

Unlike latex, oil paints dry slower but flow on the wood more smoothly. They also bond better to wood fibers. Some woods such as cedar do not accept latex easily. Cedar should be painted with oils. The cleanup has to be done with turpentine or paint thinner. Whichever paint you choose, you must first prime the wood. Priming should be done with two coats. If you want to use oil paints, use an oil primer.

When applying a paint to an exterior project, one coat is never enough. The number of coats you apply will depend on the exposure of the birdhouse. One facing north and away from the sun holds up well with three coats. One facing south should have a minimum of three coats and probably an extra one. A house facing west with a strong sun will need four coats. If it is facing east you should give it at least three coats of paint.

There are some basic painting techniques to keep in mind. Brush on even coats that are not too heavy or too thin. Make consistent, back-and-forth strokes, and watch out for drips. Check over the house for drips and missed spots before putting the brush away.

Most of us are familiar with the caulking used around tub and shower enclosures as well as doors and windows. Available in different colors, water-based caulk sticks like glue and provides a flexible, weather-resistant seal against water, dirt and insects.

Caulking is advised for outdoor birdhouses that have a lot of joined surfaces. The Victorian manor, for example, has numerous overhangs and dormers. These should be caulked prior to being painted and shingled. Caulking will keep the water out and extend the life of your project.

Safety

Birdhouse construction requires the use of tools: some power, some hand-held. Obviously it is best to exercise care when using any tool, especially those that cut. But what we often overlook are the hazards of working with the woods themselves.

Although our noses filter out some of the dust we breath and sneezing forces out more dust, particles still get trapped in the respiratory tract. Asbestos and coal dust have long been known to cause respiratory problems, but only recently has wood dust been studied as a cause of skin and eye allergies and breathing problems. Cedar, for example, has been found to be an origin of bronchitis and asthma.

Chemicals also present problems. Solvents such as turpentine, mineral spirits and lacquer thinner are skin and respiratory irritants. In the long run they can be toxic.

The best precautions are to block out and cover up. This means keeping wood dust and chemicals away from your skin. It also means wearing a respirator. Although some woodworkers prefer a simple dust mask, a good respirator serves the dual function of keeping out wood particles and harmful vapors. When working around woodworking machinery, wear ear protectors for decibel assault. Damaged eardrums may never improve. And put on goggles, even if you wear eye glasses. Keeping healthy makes woodworking all the more enjoyable.

A good beginner's project, the twin-gable house can be built in a weekend.

Twin-Gable Hide-Away: Parts List and Description

PART NUMBER	QUANTITY	SIZE	NOTES
1	1	7" by 12" by $^3/_4$"	router entrances with $^1/_2$" radius round over bit
2	1	$7^1/_4$" by 12" by $^3/_4$ "	
3	1	7" by 12" by $^3/_4$"	
4	2	$3^3/_4$" by $4^1/_4$" by $^3/_4$"	
5	1	$3^3/_4$" by 4" by $^1/_4$"	
6	4	4" by $^1/_2$" by $^1/_2$"	
7	1	4" by 12" by $^3/_4$"	
8	2	$5^1/_4$" by 7"	cedar clapboards
9	2	$4^1/_4$" by 7"	cedar clapboards, trim to fit in valley
10	2	$2^1/_4$" by $1^1/_2$" by $3^1/_4$"	bevel top edges 45 degrees on all sides
11	2	$3^1/_2$" by $^3/_8$" diameter dowel	sand end 45 degrees

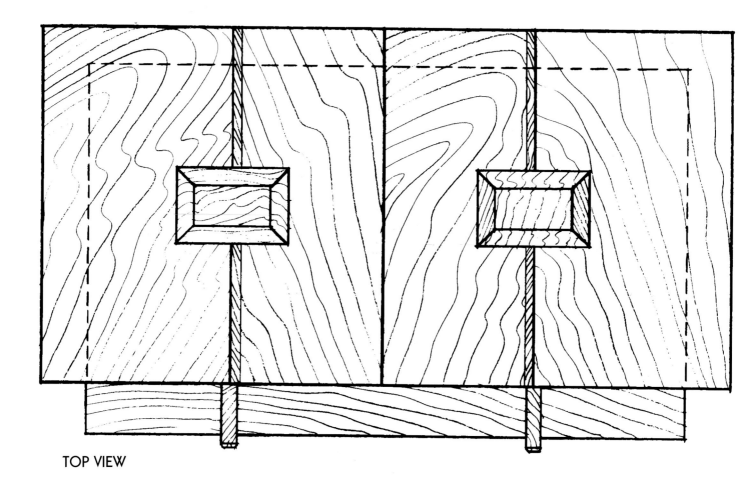

TOP VIEW

FRONT VIEW

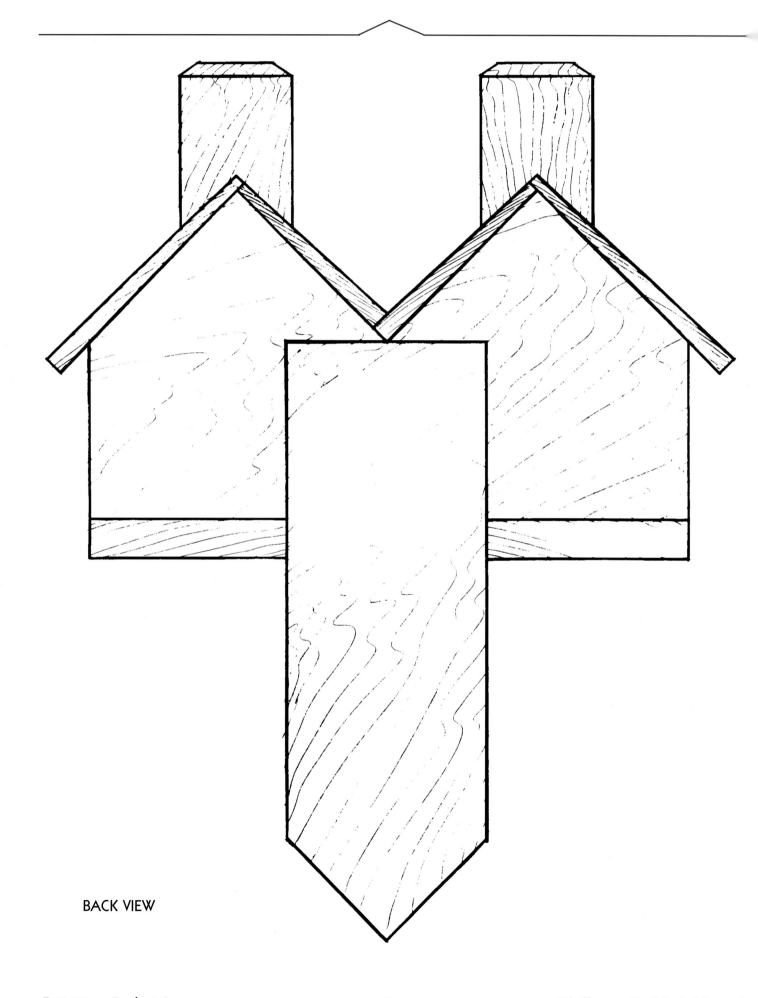

BACK VIEW

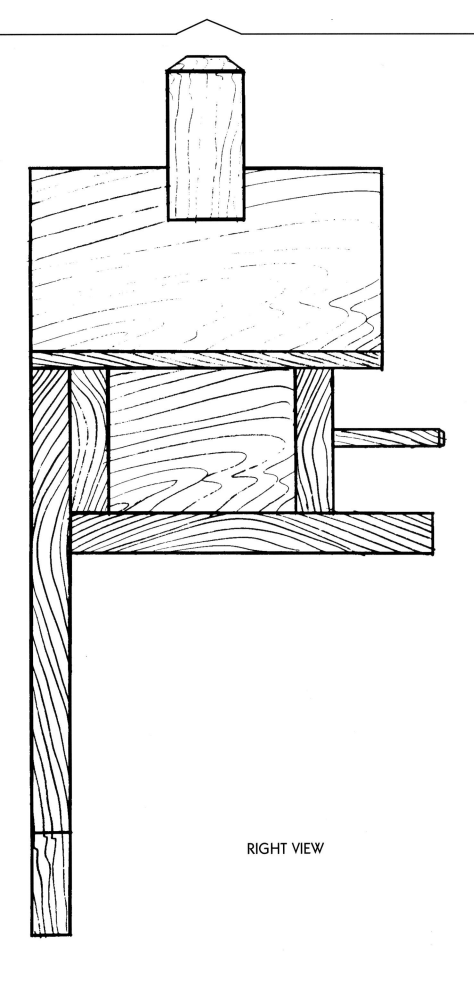

RIGHT VIEW

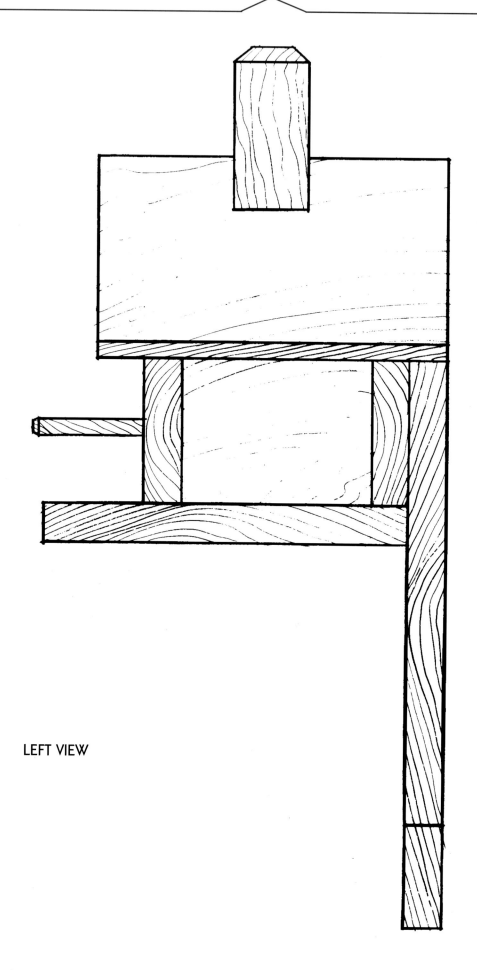

LEFT VIEW

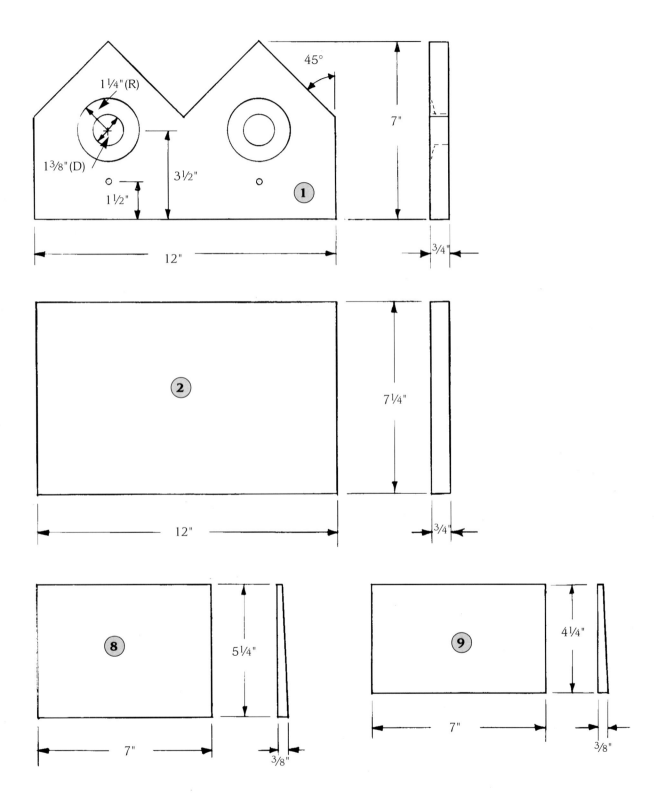

TWIN-GABLE

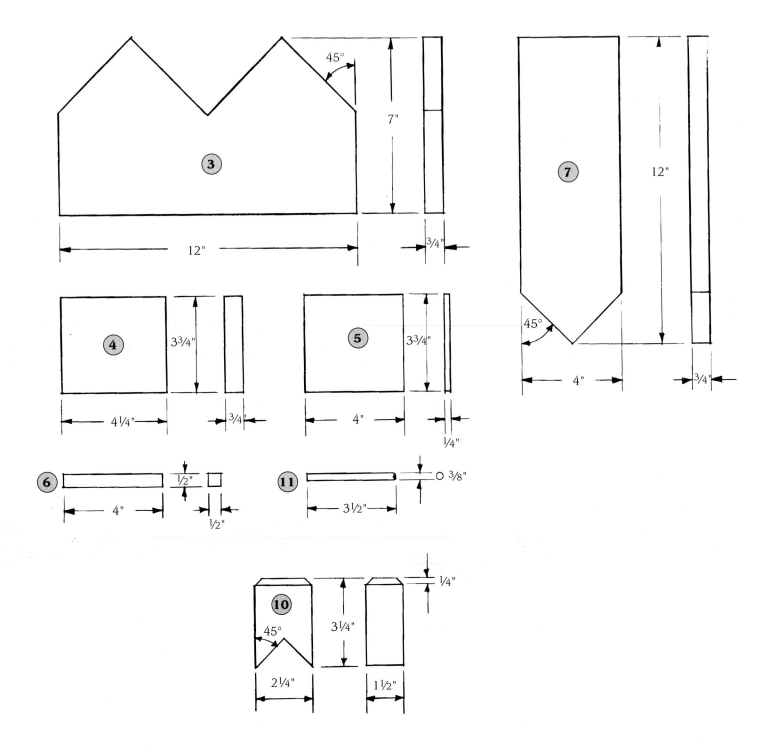

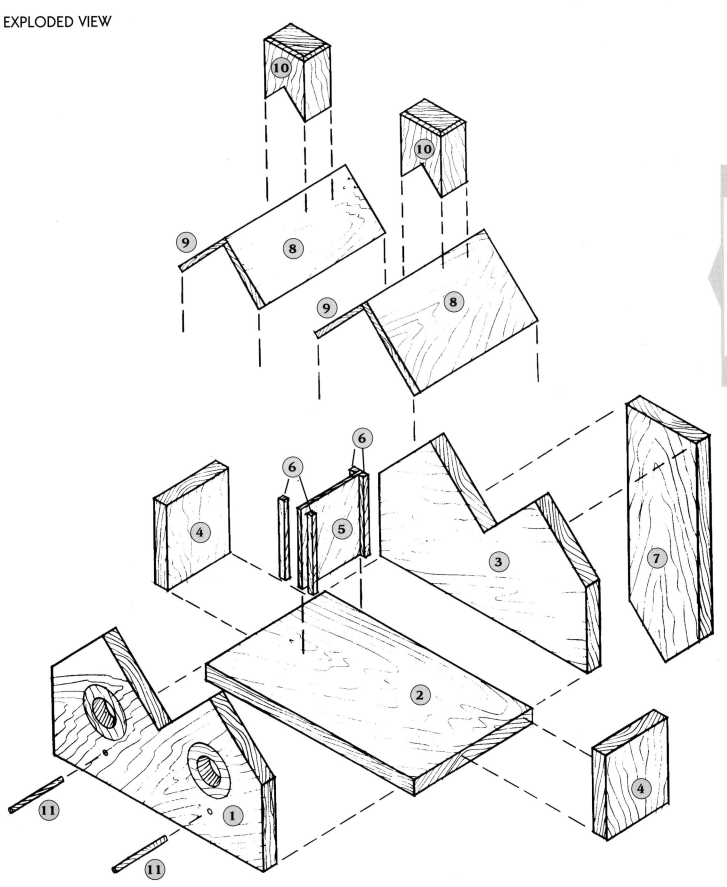

Authors' Note: Minor differences between the designer's plans and the photo how-to section will not compromise the design or the structural integrity of the birdhouses.

Project 1 Twin-Gable Hide-Away
Power Tools Used:
- Table Saw
- Band Saw
- Drill Press
- Stationary Belt Sander
- Reciprocating Spindle Sander
- Router
- Miter Saw
- Air Nailer

1 Start with a board that measures 7 inches by 12 inches for the front of the house. Mark off the points of the gables. Except for the roof, all components are made from 3/4-inch-thick lumber.

2 Draw vertical lines at these points as references for cutting and for hole placement.

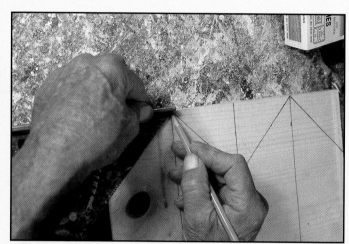

3 Use a rafter square to draw the lines that will be the roof pitches. (See Appendix A for roof pitches.)

4 Make marks across the vertical lines to indicate where the holes will be drilled.

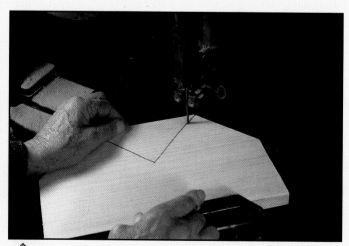

5 Cut the inverted V profiles on a band saw or with a jig saw.

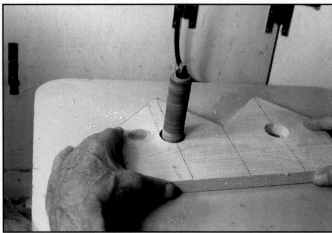

6 Use a 1³/₈-inch spade bit for the holes. A drill press gives you more control over the penetration of the bit.

7 A reciprocating spindle sander with a 1-inch-diameter drum cleans up the holes.

8 A stationary belt sander puts a smooth edge on the profiles.

9 To shape the outside edges of the holes, use a router and ¹/₂-inch radius round over bit. To prevent the bit from kicking back or tearing the wood, use a plunge router.

10 Make a back for the house using the same profile as the front but without the holes. Then go to work on the sides, which are 3³/₄ inches wide. Mark off where to cut the sides. If you measured and cut the inverted Vs correctly, the angle will be 45 degrees. Use a miter or a table saw to cut the sides. Or, you can eliminate the miter cut altogether. The roofing material will close up the interior of the house.

11 Before nailing together the sides, front and back, apply glue for a stronger bond and to keep water from seeping into the house. Use Titebond® II or another water-proof adhesive.

Birdhouse Builder's Manual

Step-by-Step • Project 1

12 Nail the front to the sides. For lots of repetitive nailing, an air-powered nail gun is a must. Use nails at least 1½ inches long.

13 Turn the assembly over and nail the back of the house in place.

14 Cut out a piece of wood measuring 3¾ inches by 4¼ inches for the divider. This gives the birdhouse two compartments of equal size. You can use ¾-inch-thick wood or ¼-inch-thick plywood held in place with cleats.

15 Nail the divider in place from the front and back.

16 Cut the bottom board to 6 inches by 10 ½ inches and nail in place. The bottom is larger than the enclosure to provide a small platform for the birds.

17 Cedar clapboards are a good choice for the roof. The wood can be purchased with one side painted as a moisture barrier. Cut the pieces so that there is an overhang on both sides.

18 Mark off where to cut the inner roof to size. Make sure the thicker part of the siding is at the lower border of the roof.

19 Nail the roof in place.

20 Cut the rest of the roof to size and nail in place.

21 Drill ³/₈-inch-diameter holes for the perches.

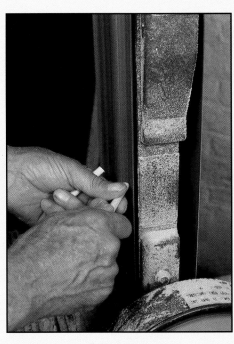

22 Put a bevel on the ends of the perch dowels using a stationary sander.

23 Apply glue to the ends of the dowels and gently tap into place.

24 The house needs a cleat for mounting it to a post or tree. Start with a board that measures 4 inches by 12 inches. Cutting a point on the bottom of the cleat adds a note of distinction to the house.

25 Use screws to secure the cleat. A driver bit in an electric drill is ergonomic.

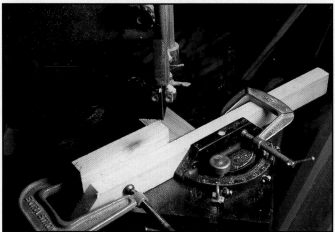

26 The house has two chimneys that are cut from 2¹/₄-inch by 1¹/₂-inch wood. A setup using a miter gauge, clamps, wood blocks and a band saw will ensure accurate notches.

27 Mark where you want to bevel the chimney tops.

28 To make the bevels quickly, bring the chimneys to the stationary sander.

29 A finished chimney, ready to be nailed in place. Your birdhouse is now complete and ready to be painted.

The rustic birdhouse brings cedar and stone together to produce a winning project.

LOG CABIN

Log Cabin: Parts List and Description

PART NUMBER	QUANTITY	SIZE	NOTES
1	9	1" by 1" by 14"	router all edges with $1/4$"-radius round over bit
2	1	6" by $10^1/2$" by $3/4$"	
3	14	1" by 1" by 6"	
4	4	1" by 1" by $4^1/4$"	
5	4	1" by 1" by $10^1/2$"	
6	1	3" by 6" by $1/4$"	
7	4	$1/2$" by $1/2$" by 6"	
8	1	6" by $6^1/4$" by $1/4$"	
9	6	1" by 1" by $9^1/4$"	
10	3	$3^1/2$" by $3/8$"-diameter dowel sand end 45 degrees	
11	2	1" by 1" by 14"	angled
12	2	1" by 1" by 12"	
13	2	1" by 1" by 10"	
14	2	1" by 1" by 8"	
15	2	1" by 1" by 6"	
16	2	1" by 1" by 4"	
17	2	1" by 1" by 2"	
18	1	$12^1/2$" by 14" by $1/4$"	
19	2	$7^1/2$" by 14"	cedar clapboards
20	2	$6^1/2$" by 14"	cedar clapboards
21	2	$1^1/2$" by 14"	cedar clapboards
22	one tube	construction adhesive	color: tan
23	130–150	small round stones $1/2$" to 1" diameter	

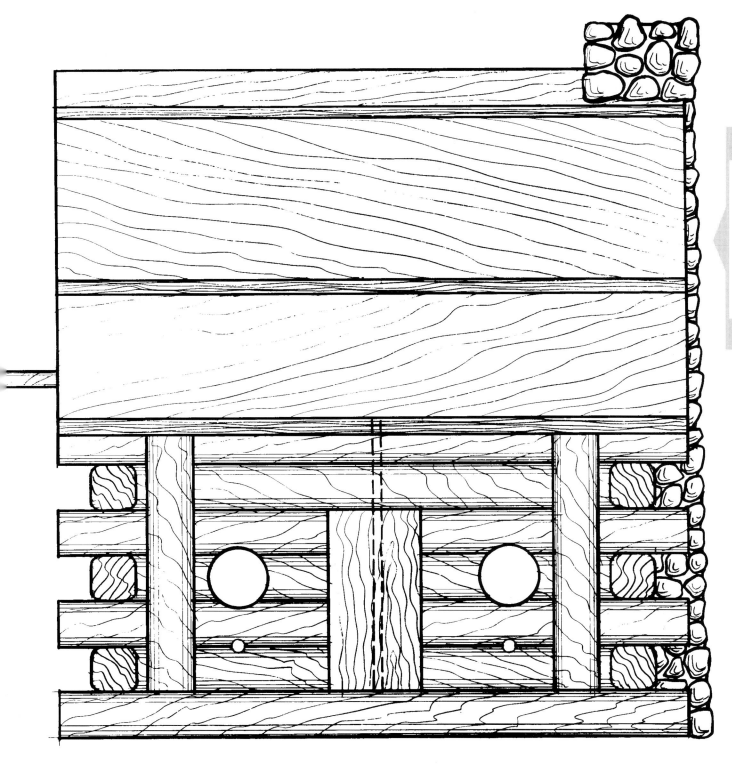

FRONT VIEW

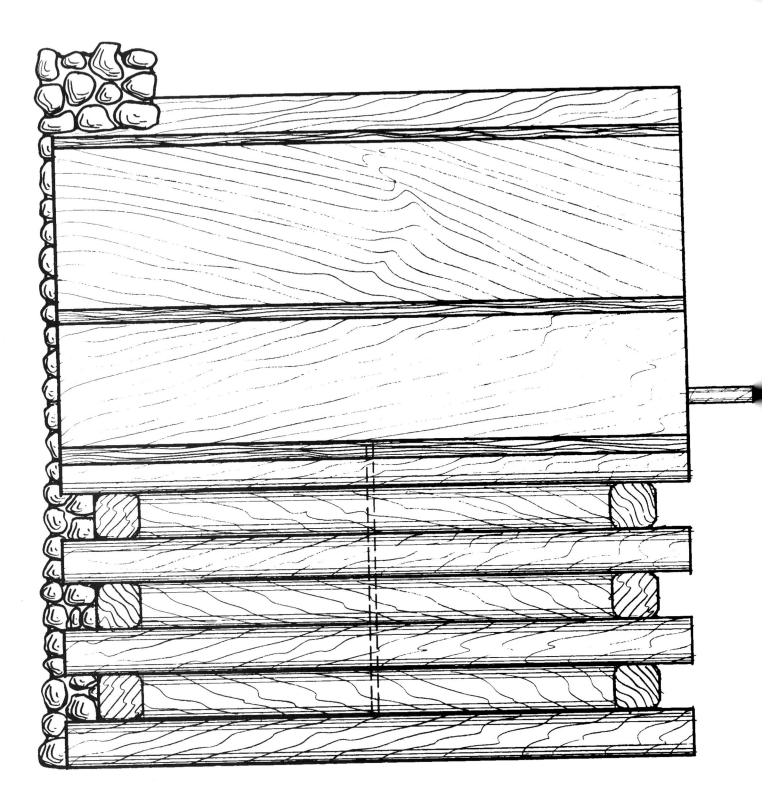

REAR VIEW

RIGHT VIEW

LEFT VIEW

BOTTOM VIEW

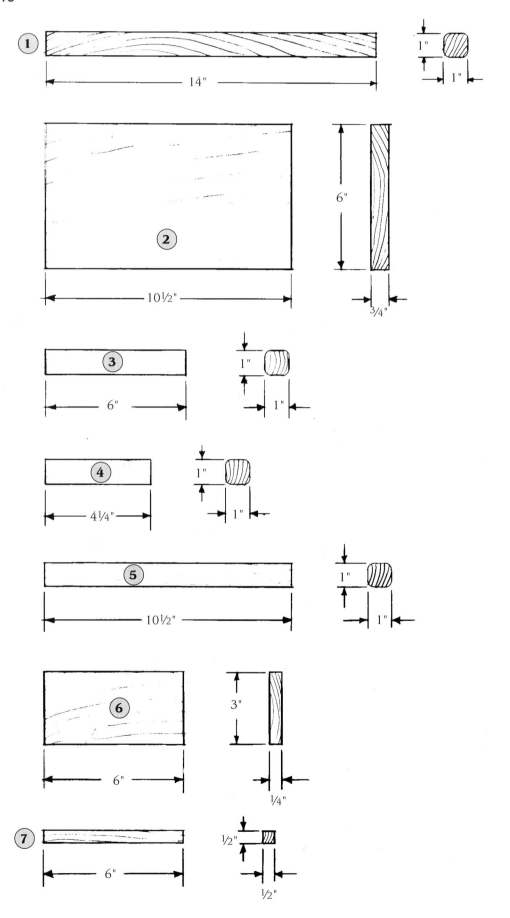

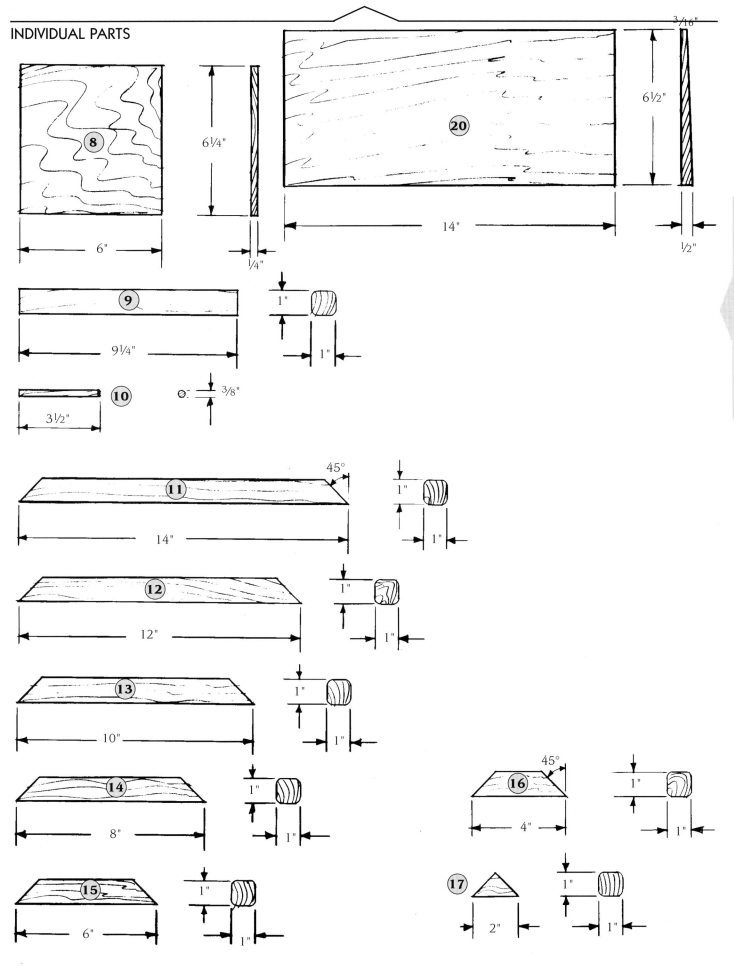

3/16"

6½"

20

14"

½"

6¼"

6"

¼"

9

9¼"

1"

1"

10

3½"

Ø

3/8"

11

45°

14"

1"

1"

12

12"

1"

1"

13

10"

1"

1"

14

8"

1"

1"

16

45°

4"

1"

1"

15

1"

6"

1"

17

2"

1"

1"

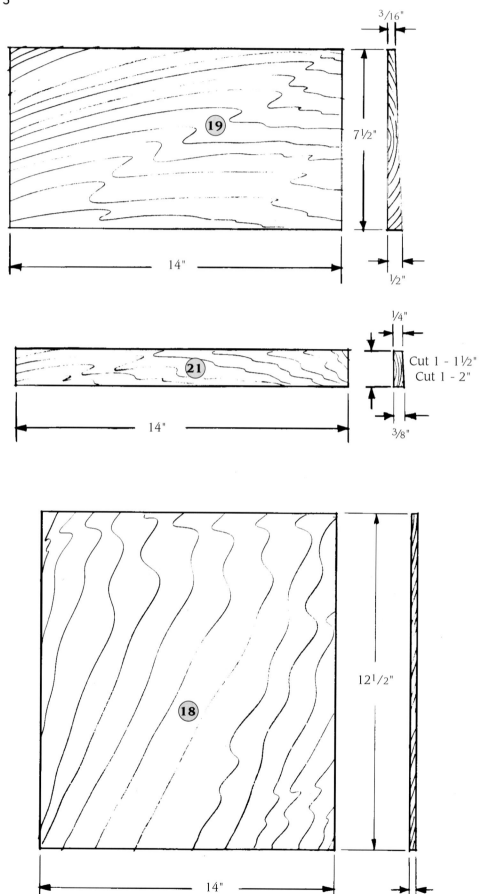

3/16"

7½"

14"

½"

¼"

21

Cut 1 - 1½"
Cut 1 - 2"

14"

3/8"

12½"

18

14"

¼"

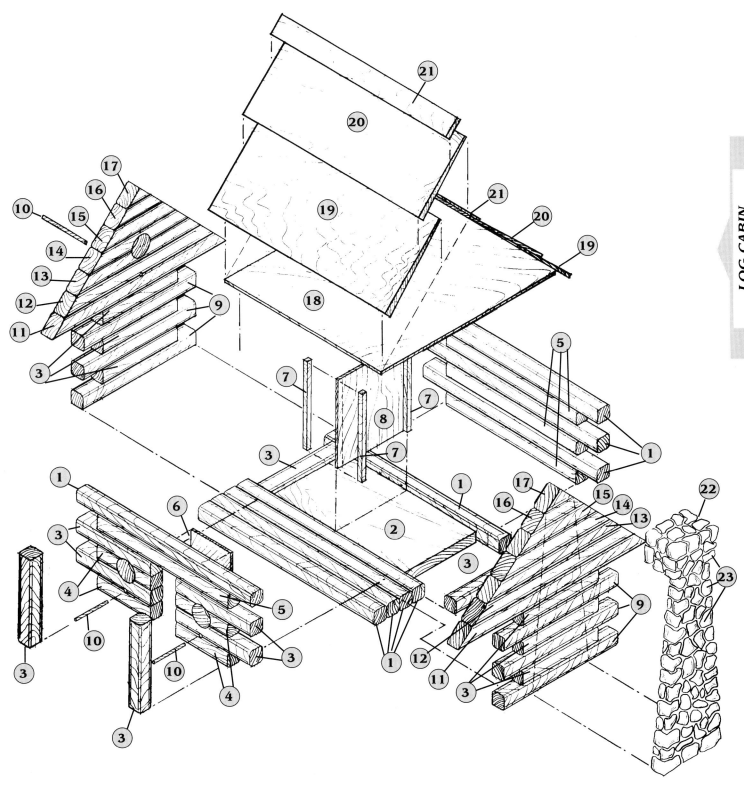

EXPLODED VIEW

Authors' Note: Minor differences between the designer's plans and the photo how-to section will not compromise the design or the structural integrity of the birdhouses.

Project 2 Log Cabin
Power Tools Used:
Table Saw
Router
Drill Press
Miter Saw
Air Nailer

1 The logs show off the best proportions if made from full 1-inch-thick stock. Cut lengths of 1-inch by 1-inch pieces depending on the base dimensions. These will be cut into long and short pieces for the walls. Round over the four edges with a 1/4-inch round over bit.

2 Cut a piece of 3/4-inch-thick stock measuring 6 inches by 10 inches for the base. Draw a centerline across its depth to center the front and back logs. Mark a centerline on two long logs. Begin by nailing a log in place on one long side of the base.

3 Nail a long log in place on the opposite side of the base.

4 Cut out lengths of logs for the sides and nail in place.

5 Nail two more logs to one side of the base. These make up part of the porch. Cut logs for the sides so that they overlap the logs for the front and back.

6 Nail the logs for the sides in place.

7 Instead of having notched logs, this house has the logs butted together at the corners. Leave an opening for the door on the porch side of the house.

8 Continue overlapping and nailing the logs in place.

9 If you cut the pieces precisely, you can work clockwise or counterclockwise as you build up the walls.

10 The door height equals four stacked logs. Another log caps the top of the doorway.

11 Use a 1³/₈-inch spade bit to drill out the holes centered on each side of the door. Drill a hole into the gable end opposite the chimney.

12 Add an additional log for the porch.

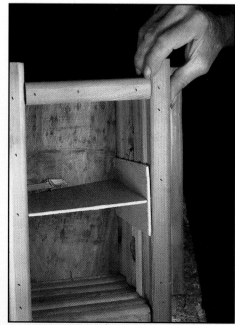

13 A partition for the interior of the cabin can be as simple as 1/4-inch-thick plywood held in place with "wedges" of the same material. One of these wedges provides a covering for the door opening. An alternative is to nail retaining strips or cleats to the walls and slide the partition in place. If you do this, make sure that the door opening is sealed.

14 Begin work on the gable ends. They will have an overhang to accommodate posts for the porch. After laying seven logs next to each other, use a rafter square to draw the 45-degree pitch angle.

15 Make sure the pitch line is dark enough to see.

16 You can use a miter saw to cut the logs, but it is safer not to cut all seven at the same time.

17 Build up the ends one log at a time.

18 Continue adding one log on top of another.

19 The gables are topped with very small pieces of wood. For safety, cut the top piece on a band saw.

20 Build up the other gable end one piece at a time.

21 The cabin needs a ceiling to enclose the two compartments and to provide an overhang to support the porch posts. Cut the ceiling to size on a table saw or with a saber saw.

22 When fitting the ceiling, make sure it does not extend beyond the logs in the rear. If it does, it will prevent the roof from having a tight fit.

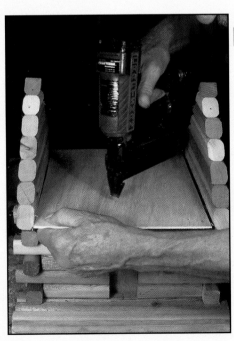

23 Nail the ceiling in place.

24 To make the porch posts, use the same log stock. Nail in place through the ceiling.

25 Nail the posts from underneath the porch.

26 Before securing the roof, check that the gable ends are perpendicular to the ceiling.

27 Cedar clapboards, left unpainted, are ideal for a log cabin. Cut the pieces to size so that they overhang the ends of the cabin, then scribe lines where the nails will make contact with the gable ends.

28 Nail the clapboards in place.

29 Overlap the first piece of clapboard with another, bringing the second piece right to the peak.

30 To keep water out, cap the ridge with small pieces of clapboard.

31 Glue and gently hammer a 3/8-inch-diameter dowel below the hole in the gable end. Put 3/8-inch dowels under the holes in the front.

32 The other side of the cabin has a stone chimney. Draw the sides of the chimney using a pencil and straight edge.

33 To add some interest to the house, taper the sides of the chimney.

34 Use a variety of different size stones. Since it is hard to judge how many you will need, collect at least a coffee can full.

35 Apply a thick layer of construction adhesive over the entire area. Work a section at a time. Lay the cabin on its side so you have a horizontal surface on which to work. Otherwise, the stones may shift and pull away from the adhesive.

37 Continue cementing stones, working a small area at a time.

36 Begin at the bottom, laying the stones out one at a time. Work the stones into the adhesive for a strong bond.

38 When the adhesive has had a chance to set up, stand the cabin upright and build up the chimney. It is not necessary to cut a notch in the roof overhang.

39 As the adhesive is drying, there is still enough flexibility to mold the chimney shape with your hands.

40 Add adhesive to the top of the chimney and build up its height with more stones.

41 The chimney is finished. Allow it to set up overnight. This house is ready to be mounted on a post.

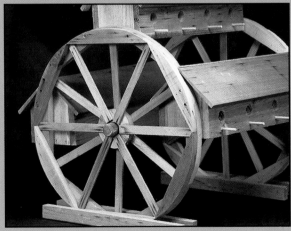

The wagon wheels project is sure to be an eye catcher.

WAGON WHEELS

Wagon Wheels: Parts List and Description

PART NUMBER	QUANTITY	SIZE	NOTES
1	4	1" by 1^3/4" by 21"	
2	24	1" by 1^5/8" by 12"	12" radius
3	24	1" by ^{1}/4" by 11"	
4	4	1^1/2" diameter by 2"	1^1/2" exposed each side
5	2	5" diameter by 1"	cut hole in center 1^1/2" diameter
6	3	5^1/4" by 24" by ^{3}/4"	drill 1^3/8" holes for entrance
7	3	5^1/2" by 24" by ^{3}/4"	
8	3	5^1/4" by 24" by ^{3}/4"	45 degree top edge
9	6	8" by 5^1/2" by ^{3}/4"	
10	9	7^1/4" by 5^1/2" by ^{3}/4"	
11	3	6^1/4" by 26" by ^{1}/2"	clapboards
12	1	6" by 26" by ^{1}/2"	clapboards
13	2	6" by 26" by ^{1}/2"	clapboards, cut notch to fit wheel
14	12	3" by ^{1}/4" galvanized screws	
15	12	2^3/4" by ^{3}/8" diameter dowels	

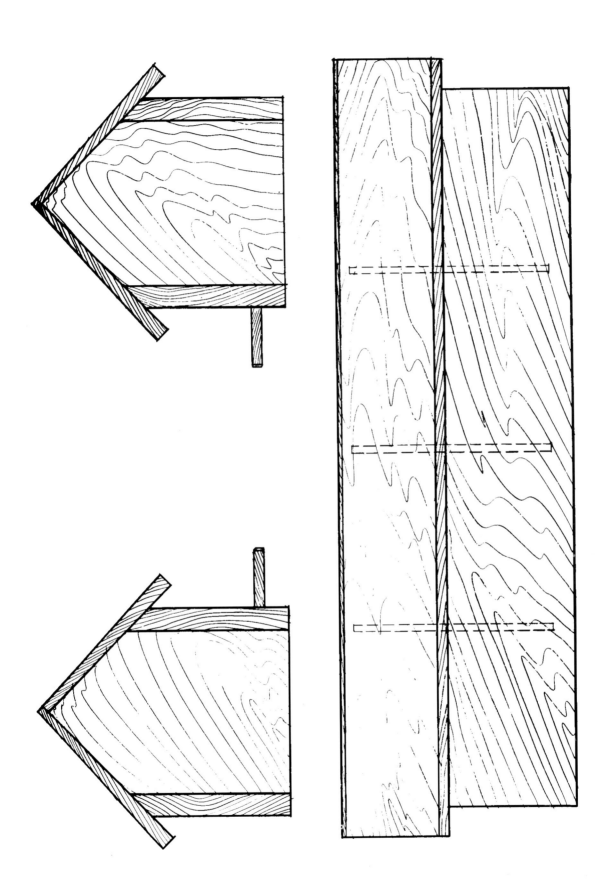

BACK VIEW, RIGHT, LEFT

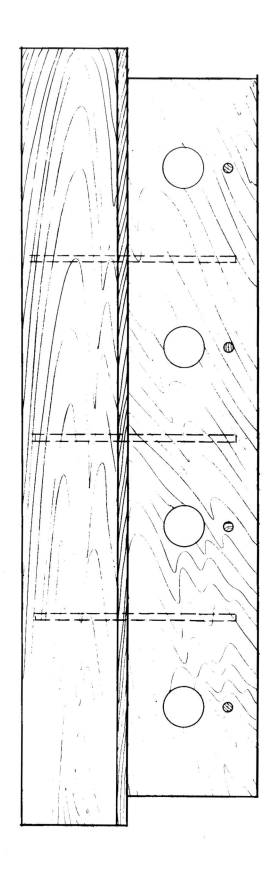

FRONT VIEW

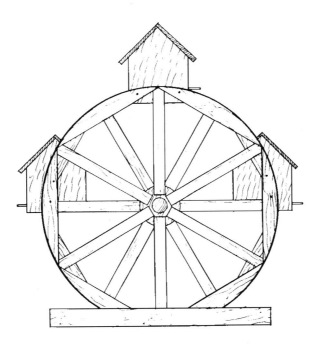

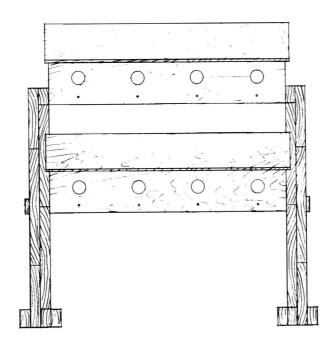

SIDE VIEW

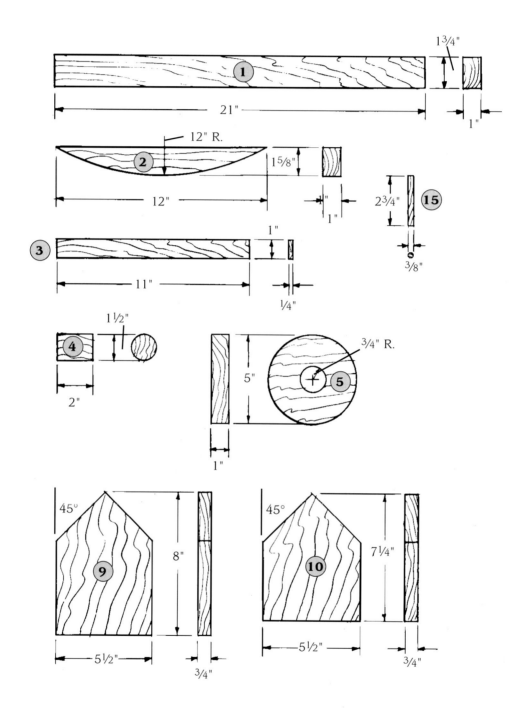

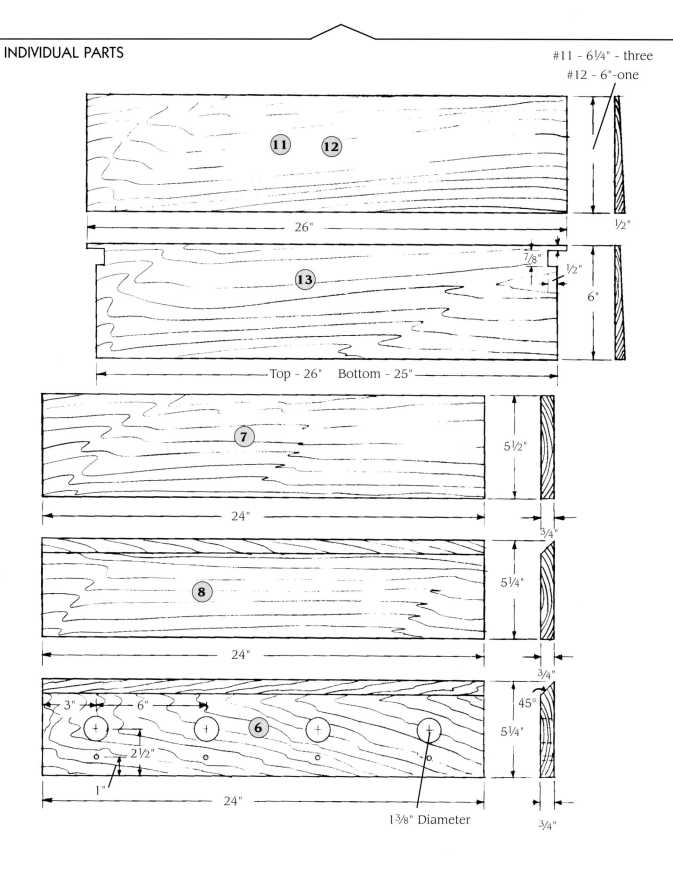

#11 - 6¼" - three
#12 - 6"-one

26"

½"

7/8"   ½"   6"

Top - 26"   Bottom - 25"

5½"

24"   ¾"

5¼"

24"   ¾"

3"   6"

45°

5¼"

2½"

1"

24"   ¾"

1⅜" Diameter

WAGON WHEELS

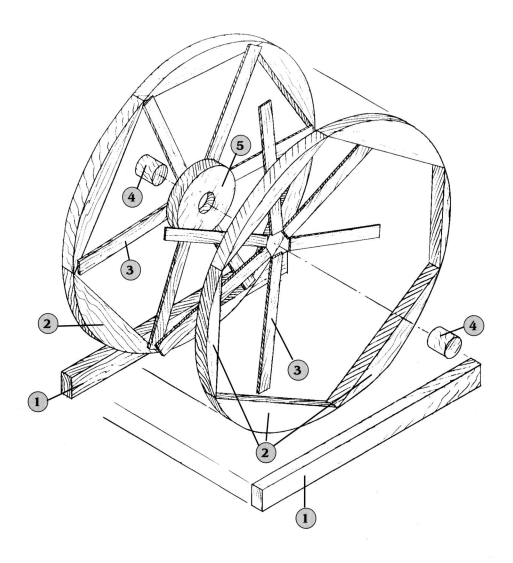

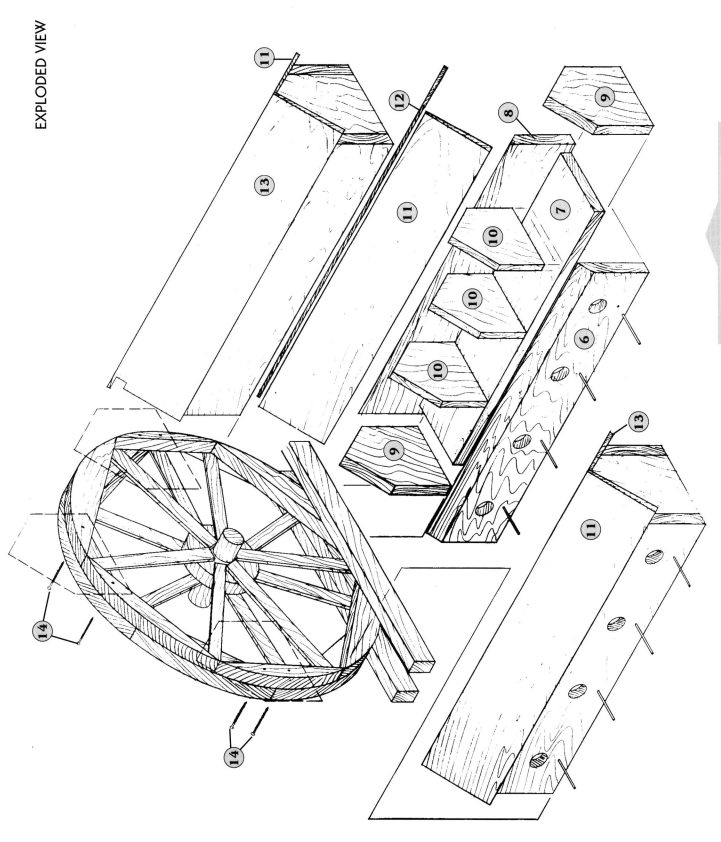

Project 3 Wagon Wheels

Power Tools Used:
- Table Saw
- Band Saw
- Stationary Belt Sander
- Drill Press
- Miter Saw

1 Each wheel rim consists of two overlapping circles of wood. Each circle consists of six separate "arcs" of wood. Use a piece of plywood at least 24 inches square for a template. Start by dividing the template board into quarters. Then use a 30- to 60-degree draftsman's triangle to divide each quarter into thirds. Draw a 24-inch-diameter circle and connect the points where the lines intersect the circle. You should have two overlapping hexagons.

2 Cut out six pieces of 1-inch-thick by 1⅝-inch-wide boards as long as the side of a hexagon. Lay out the boards and draw the 24-inch-diameter circle on their faces.

3 The same layout can be done with the overlapping pieces.

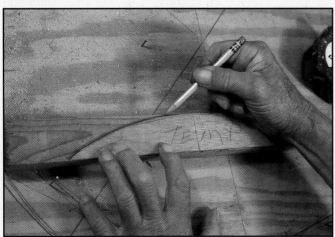

4 If your layout has been accurate, and all sides of both hexagons are equal in length, then you can use a single template to cut out all 12 pieces.

5 Cut out the arcs on a band saw.

6 Use a stationary belt sander to smooth the bandsawed wood.

7 Use a narrow stationary belt sander to slightly round over the edges of the arcs.

8 If you want to save the original template board from wear and tear and use it again, prepare a piece of scrap plywood for assembly.

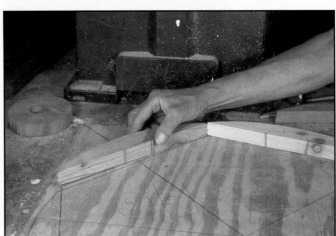

9 Lay out one arc at a time so that they just touch.

10 Six pieces make up one face of the rim.

11 Before assembling the other face of the rim, mark off a centerline on each arc.

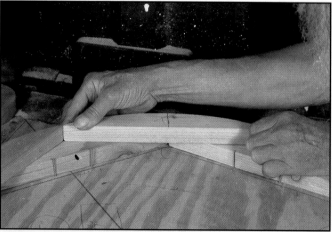

12 As you lay out the arcs, match up the centerline (marked off in the previous step) with where the previous arcs touch.

13 You may end up with a gap between two of the arcs.

14 To close up the gap in the previous step, use the template from the first step to make a new arc that is slightly longer.

15 The rim pieces are assembled prior to being nailed together.

16 The wheel has a 1-inch-thick hub that holds the rim and spokes together. Draw a 5-inch-diameter circle for the hub and a 1½-inch-diameter circle for the axle hole.

17 Band saw the hub to shape.

18 Use a spade bit to drill out the axle hole.

19 Clean up the axle hole with a spindle sander.

20 Return to the rim and nail the arcs together. Make sure the nails do not go through to the plywood template.

21 Each face of the rim has six spokes made from 1/4-inch-thick by 1-inch-wide lumber. Each needs to be miter cut to fit where the arcs touch.

22 Mark off the length of the spokes using the fixed hub as the reference.

23 The miter saw quickly cuts stacked pieces of the same size wood.

24 Clean up the mitered ends of the spokes on the stationary sander.

25 Do a trial layout of the spokes.

26 Mark off where the spokes rest on the hub.

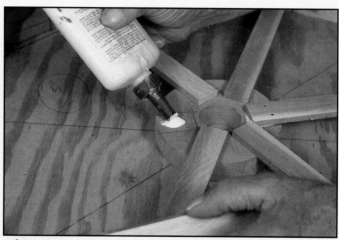

27 Remove the spokes and apply glue.

28 Nail the spokes in place.

29 Turn the wheel over and repeat the previous steps of laying out spokes and cutting them to size.

30 Put a bevel on a 1½-inch-diameter dowel for the axle.

31 Fit the axle in place.

32 Since it is unlikely that the two faces of the rim will be perfectly round, sand the assembly on the stationary belt sander.

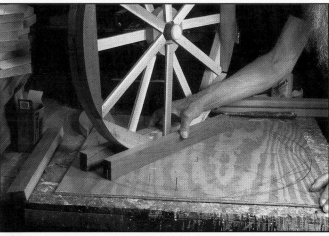

33 Supports on the wheels do two things: They allow the assembly to be mounted to a platform and they keep the wheels from rotating when they are attached to the houses. Use 1-inch-thick by 1¾-inch-wide by 21-inch-long lumber.

34 Nail one support on each side.

35 The wheel stands on its own.

36 Work begins on the three houses by cutting the ends to size. Each gable end has a 45-degree pitch.

37 Fit the ends to a base, which measures 5½ inches by 24 inches.

38 The front and back need to be beveled at a 45-degree angle to match the gable pitch.

39 Before I cut the 45-degree angle for the front and back, I put four 1⅜-inch-diameter holes on the front.

40 After nailing the sides, front, back and base together, cut out three partitions and space them equally inside the house.

41 Draw reference lines on the front and back and nail the partitions in place.

42 Drill ³/₈-inch-diameter holes for perches.

43 Glue and gently tap the perches in place.

44 Use cedar clapboards for the roof. Use a single piece for each side. Mark where to trim the wood.

45 Scribe a reference line for nailing.

46 Nail the clapboards in place.

47 Assembly of the houses and wheels can be difficult for one person. One approach is to give support to each house and clamp the assembly together.

48 Notch the roofs of the two houses where they overlap the wheels slightly. Use a saber saw to cut the notches.

49 Assembly is easier if another person supports each house at its center and keeps it level.

50 Use 3-inch-long deck or galvanized screws to secure the houses to the wheels. Also, note how the roof of the house overlaps the wheel rim. Once the three houses are in place, the homestead is ready to be mounted on a platform.

The Victorian manor is sure to appeal to the woodworker looking for a challenge.

Victorian Manor: Parts List and Description

PART NUMBER	QUANTITY	SIZE	NOTES
1	1	35" by 11" by $3/4$"	
2	2	11" by 12" by $3/4$"	
3	2	$14^1/2$" by 12" by $3/4$"	
4	2	37" long	embossed molding, 45 degree ends
5	2	13" long	embossed molding, 45 degree ends
6	2	$13^1/2$" by $1/2$" by $1/2$"	cleats
7	2	$9^1/2$" by $1/2$" by $1/2$"	cleats
8	16	$2^1/2$" by $1/2$" by $1/2$"	
9	16	$2^1/2$" high	casing molding
10	16	$2^5/8$" by $2^1/2$" by $1/2$"	45 degree both ends
11	16	$5/8$" by $2^5/8$" by $1/8$"	45 degree both ends
12	16	$1/4$" by $2^5/8$" by $1/8$"	45 degree both ends
13	40	3" by 2"	asphalt shingles
14	8	$2^1/2$" by $3/8$" diameter	dowel
15	2	28" long	crown molding
16	8	3" by 3" by $1/4$"	drill entrance holes
17	2	$3^1/2$" by 11" by $3/4$"	
18	2	$2^1/4$ " by 11" by $3/4$"	
19	2	16" long	crown molding
20	2	$5^1/2$" by 4" by 1"	router edge with $1/2$" round over
21	2	$7^1/2$" by $3^3/4$" by 1"	router top edge with $1/2$" round over bit
22	24	2" by 2" by $3/4$"	45 degree sides $1/4$" down all sides, drill out center $1^1/4$" diameter, $1/4$" deep
23	8	11" by $1^1/4$" diameter	fluted, 12 ribs per column
24	4	8" by $1^1/4$" diameter	fluted, 12 ribs per column
25	1	$14^1/2$" by $3^3/4$" by $1/4$"	
26	1	$14^1/2$" by $9^1/2$" by $1/4$"	
27	1	$14^1/2$" by 6" by $1/4$"	
28	2	$32^1/2$" by $16^1/2$" by $1/4$"	
29	1	$32^1/2$" by $16^1/2$" by $3/4$"	
30	1	$16^1/2$" by $8^1/4$" by $3/4$"	
31	8	7" by $1/2$" by $1/2$"	
32	2	7" by $1/4$" by 8"	
33	2	$16^1/2$" by $8^1/4$" by $3/4$"	drill $1^3/8$" diameter entrance holes
34	2	$16^1/2$" by 4" by $3/4$	
35	2	$16^1/2$" long	dentil molding
36	2	$16^1/2$" long	embossed molding
37	2	$3/8$" diameter by $2^1/2$"	dowel
38	2	$13^3/4$" by 36" by $3/4$" – 1 13" by 36" by $3/4$" – 1	overlap at top
39	4	14" long	screen molding
40	4	$4^1/2$" by 5" by $3/4$"	
41	8	$3^1/2$" by $3^1/2$" by $3/4$"	
42	8	$2^1/2$" by $1/2$" by $1/2$"	

Victorian Manor: Parts List and Description (continued)

43	8	$2^1/2$" long	casing molding
44	8	5" by $^7/8$" by $^1/8$"	
45	8	5" by $^1/4$" by $^1/8$"	
46	4	$^3/8$" diameter by $2^1/2$"	dowel
47	8	5" by 7" by $^3/4$"	
48	24	$^1/2$" diameter by $1^7/8$"	standard turnings
49	40	8" by 2"	asphalt shingles
50	2	$3^1/2$" by $10^1/2$" by $^1/2$"	cut out center
51	2	$2^1/2$" by $4^1/8$" by $^1/2$"	
52	4	$4^1/2$" by $1^5/8$" by $^1/2$"	
53	4	$6^1/2$" long	embossed molding
54	1	$^1/2$" by $2^1/2$" by $2^1/2$"	
55	1	$1^1/2$ diameter bell, 1" high with open screw hook	
56	1	1" by $2^1/2$" by $2^1/2$"	
57	4	$4^1/2$" by $2^3/8$" by $^1/2$"	
58	4	$5^1/2$" by $1^1/2$" by $^1/2$"	dentil molding
59	4	6" long	nose and cove molding
60	4	$6^1/2$" long	embossed molding
61	1	$5^1/2$" by $5^1/2$" by $^1/2$"	
62	1	$2^1/2$" by $2^1/2$" by 7"	
63	4	$3^1/2$" long	embossed molding
64	1	$^1/2$" diameter by $1^1/2$" high	standard turning for peak
65	4	$^1/2$" diameter by $1^1/4$" high	standard turning
66	30	40" by 2"	asphalt shingles

FRONT AND BACK VIEW

RIGHT AND LEFT VIEW

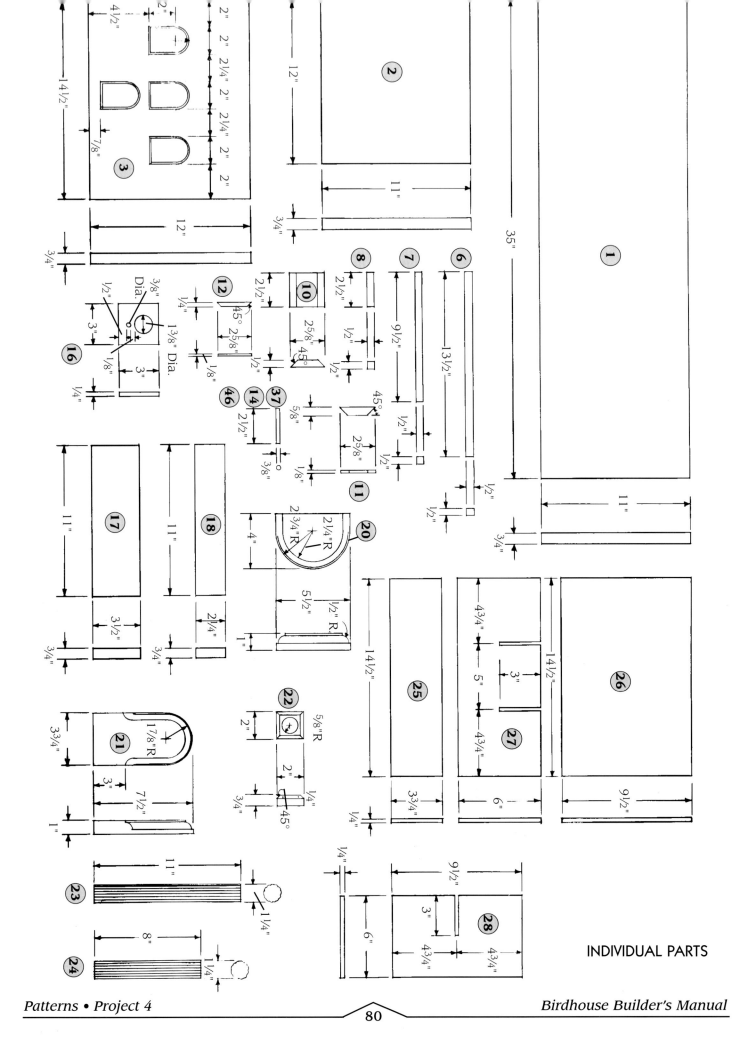

INDIVIDUAL PARTS

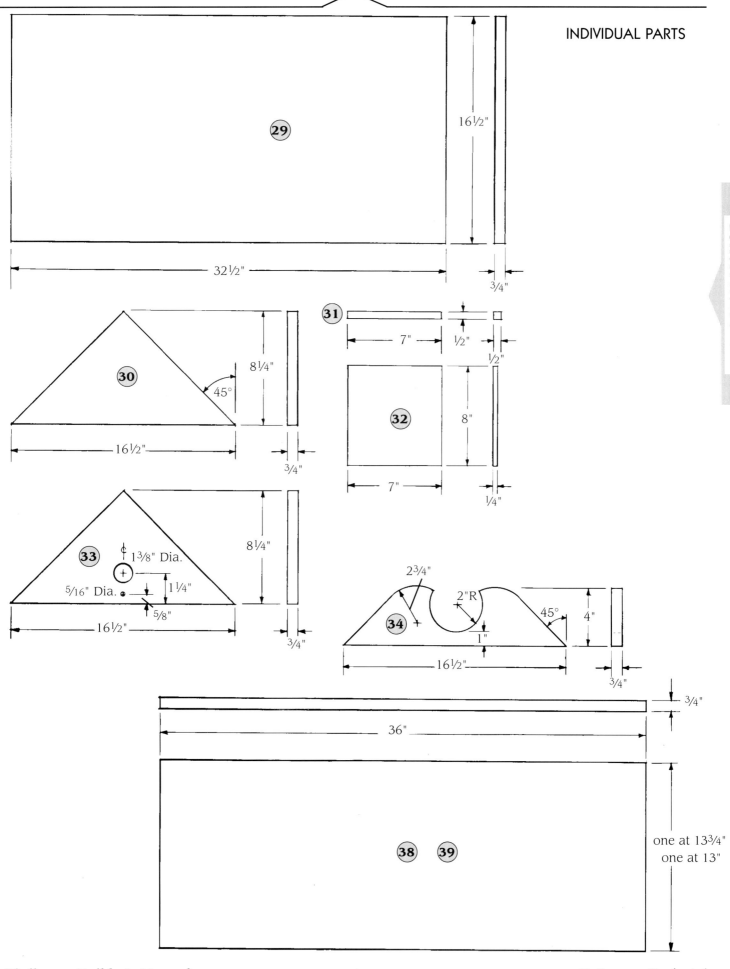

29

16½"

32½"

¾"

30

8¼"

45°

16½"

¾"

31

7"

½"

½"

32

8"

7"

¼"

33

1⅜" Dia.

5/16" Dia.

1¼"

5/8"

8¼"

16½"

¾"

34

2¾"

2"R

1"

45°

4"

16½"

¾"

¾"

36"

38   39

one at 13¾"
one at 13"

INDIVIDUAL PARTS

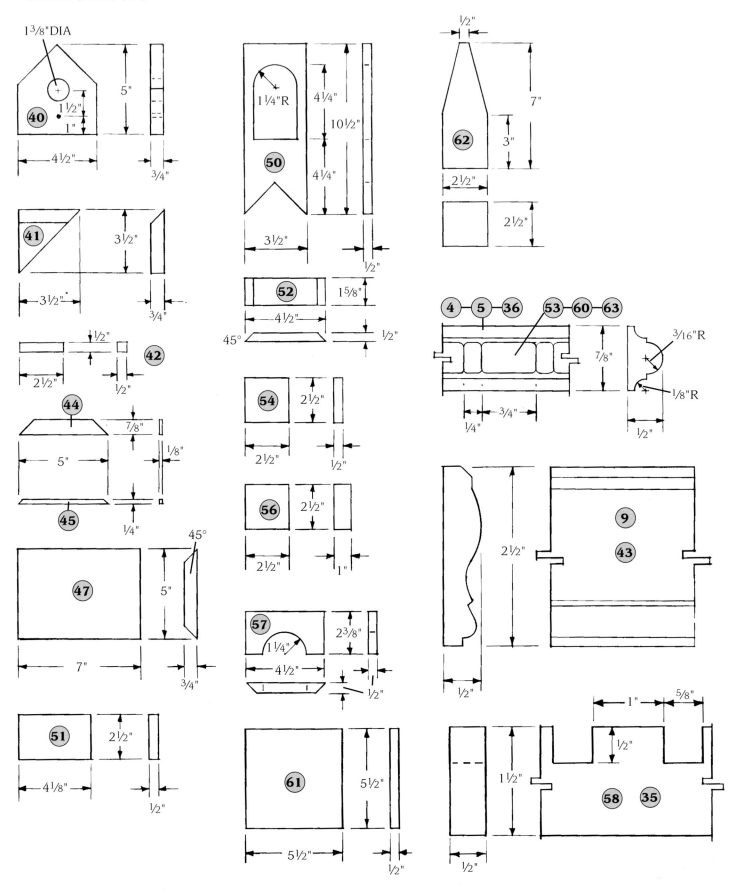

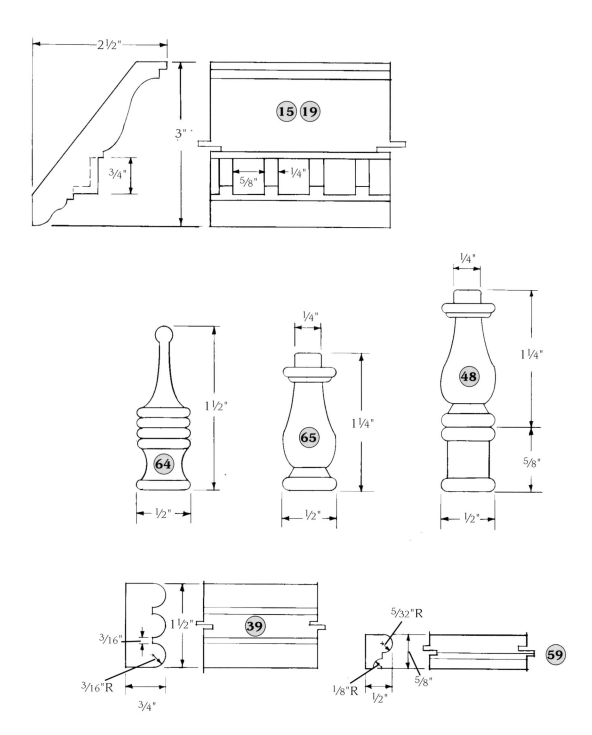

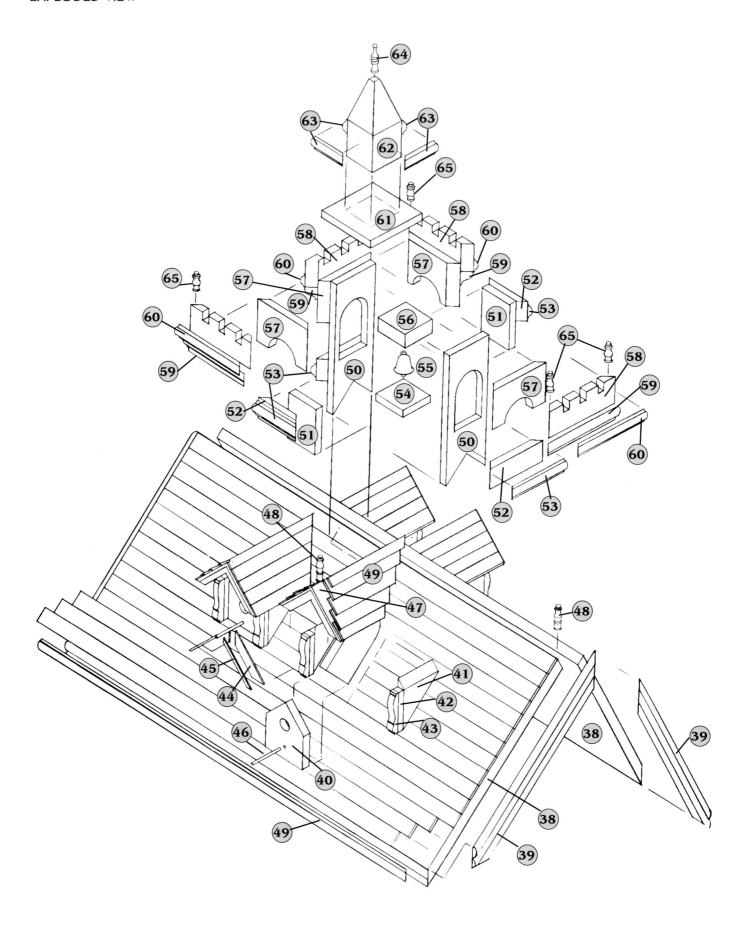

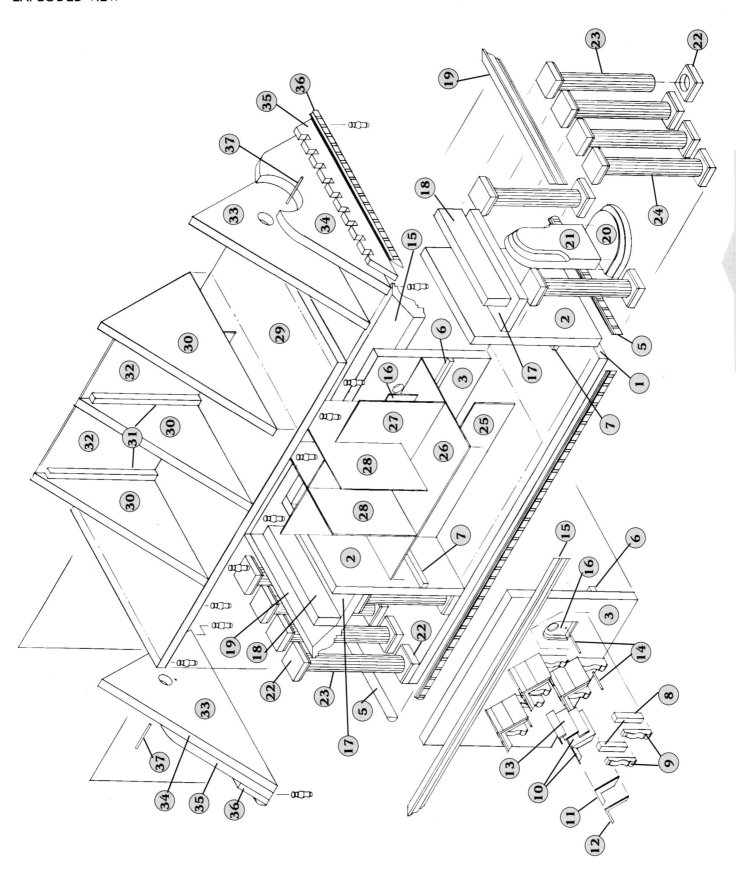

VICTORIAN MANOR

Project 4 Victorian Manor

Power Tools Used:

Table Saw
Drill Press
Band Saw
Miter Saw
Router
Air Nailer

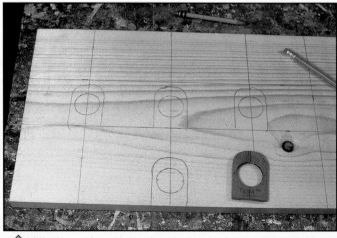

1 Work on the manor begins with the two fronts that measure 14¼ inches by 12 inches. Each has one door and four window openings with rounded tops. Use a template to lay them out.

2 Use a saber saw to cut out the openings.

3 Round over the openings with a ¼-inch round over bit.

4 The inside of the two fronts are faced with ¼-inch-thick plywood. These have holes that are located in the door and window openings. Use a 1⅜-inch spade bit. You can also use smaller pieces of plywood and cover each opening.

5 A floor divides the house into upper and lower levels. Nail a strip in place to support the floor.

6 Make sure the holes line up with the openings in the two fronts.

7 Nail the plywood in place.

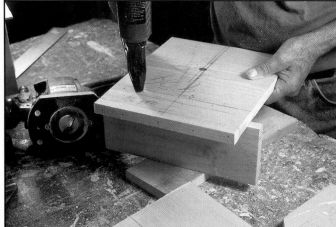

8 The sides are boxed out with pieces of wood to create an overhang or soffit.

9 Glue and nail the two fronts in place.

10 Secure the walls to the base with nails.

11 Next use screws to join the base to the walls. Deck screws work well.

12 The lower floor of the manor is divided into two compartments. Use plywood for the wall.

13 Cut to size a piece of plywood to create a ceiling for the lower level.

14 The upper floor of the house has six compartments, three for each front. The compartments are made using partition joints. Engage the partitions by halving the cross pieces.

15 A quick way to secure the partitions is to wedge them in place with a shim. Partitions can also be held in place with cleats.

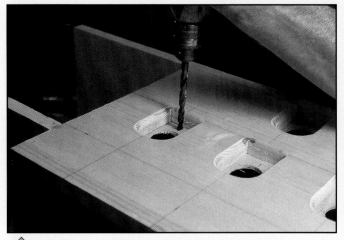

Drill 3/8-inch-diameter holes for the perches.

16

Glue and tap 3/8-inch dowels in place.

17

18 Each window and door has an overhang. Pre-drill holes and nail them in place.

19 Face the overhangs with 1/8-inch-thick pieces of wood. These cover the end grain of the overhangs. Paint will not seal up end grain easily, and the grain can deteriorate more quickly than surface or edge grain.

20 Use pieces of casing molding to decorate the sides of the door and window openings.

21 Check that all overhangs and moldings line up and maintain their symmetry.

22 Each side has decorative pieces added for interest. The parts are contoured with a router bit. Nail the pieces in place.

23 The sides are decorated with six fluted columns: four in the front and two near the wall. Each column has a capital and base for top and bottom. The capitals and bases are pre-drilled to accept the columns and one edge is rounded over.

24 Nail the columns, capitals and bases in place.

25 A ceiling board is placed on top of the walls. Its dimensions are determined by the size of the molding used. This is a combination crown and dentil molding.

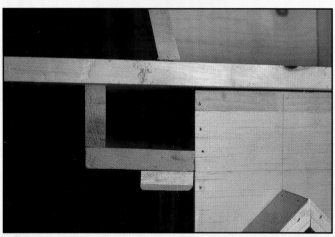

26 Once the ceiling is in place, a board is cut to size and nailed between the ceiling and the overhang or soffit.

27 Five pieces of wood are cut to size and located on the ceiling. These make up the gable ends and partitions that provide more compartments to the manor. Four are in place here. The fifth will be placed on the remaining gable end.

28 Two interior compartments are divided in half. Openings on either side of the roof provide access.

29 The gable ends have openings and pediment-shaped trim.

30 Use screws to secure the roof to the gables and partitions. Locate the positions of the dormers over the compartments.

31 Before the dormers are put in place, use a 2½-inch-diameter hole saw to make the openings. These are oversized because the angle of the roof and the small size of the dormers require more room for a bird to maneuver. You can also use a saber saw and cut out square or rectangular openings.

32 A compound angle is required where the dormer roof joins the main roof. Plus, a 45-degree angle has to be cut at the peak and eave of each side of a dormer roof. Use a protractor to help lay out the compound angle before cutting. Do not be too concerned if the roofs do not fit perfectly. They are caulked and covered with asphalt shingles later on.

34 Cut the eave at a 45-degree angle.

33 Set the saw at a 30-degree angle and the table saw miter gauge at a 35-degree angle.

35 Cut the peak at a 45-degree angle.

36 To cut the opposite half of the dormer roof, put the miter gauge on the opposite side of the blade. Set the miter gauge at 35 degrees and the blade at 30 degrees.

37 The fronts of the dormers require a 45-degree pitch and a 45-degree bevel at their bases to conform to the roof. Use a miter saw if you feel comfortable cutting small pieces on it. A band saw is a safer tool.

38 Glue up each dormer front with the two sides.

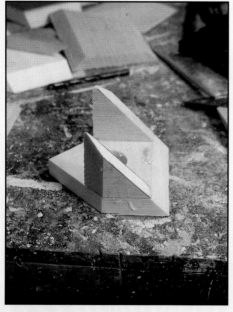

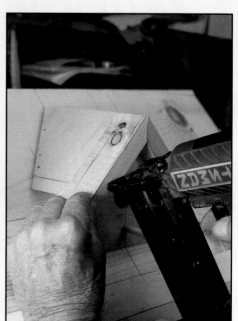

39 Use a rafter square to position the dormers and nail in place.

40 Nail the dormer roofs in place.

41 Nail thin strips of wood over the edges of the dormer roofs. Glue and insert dowels for the perches.

42 Use the miter saw to cut the crown and dentil molding to size.

43 Nail the crown and dentil molding in place.

44 Trim the corners of the mansion with embossed molding.

45 Use the same embossed molding to trim the base of the manor.

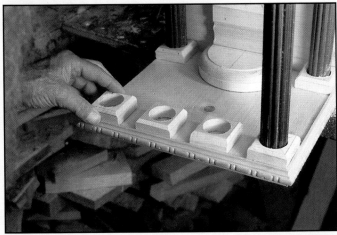

46 Locate the four columns on each side of the mansion using the bases as reference.

47 Use a small level and check that each column is perpendicular to the base.

48 Nail the columns in place from underneath the base.

49 Nail the capitals in place.

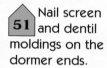

51 Nail screen and dentil moldings on the dormer ends.

50 Cut out pieces of casing molding to trim the dormer fronts.

52 Begin work on the cupola by gluing up a box and cutting out a notch so it can rest on the roof. Frame the tower base with 1/2-inch-thick wood.

53 Continue building the walls using 1/2-inch-thick wood. The cupola consists of four arched openings.

54 Glue the arches in place for the remaining two sides. Nail all the pieces together.

55 Frame the upper portion of the tower with 1/2-inch-thick lumber. Use bevel cuts to join the corners.

56 Scribe lines for the arches on the molding cut in the previous step.

57 Cap the tower framework with 1/2-inch-thick pieces of wood.

58 Sand flush the edges of the wood that were added in the previous step.

59 Apply dentil, nose and cove, and embossed moldings to the tower framework.

60 Cut the steeple to shape on a band saw. After you cut away a side, reattach it with double-sided tape. When you saw away the opposite side, the steeple profile will not be distorted.

61 Sand away the band saw marks using the stationary sander.

62 The bell tower, once finished, is put aside until the roof is shingled.

63 Use asphalt shingles for the roof. Cut strips using a sheet rock knife and a steel T-square.

64 Use the first strip that you cut as a template for cutting the rest of the strips.

65 A heavy duty paper cutter quickly cuts the strips to size.

VICTORIAN MANOR

66 Nail the strips to the roof, starting at the bottom.

67 Use a piece of scrap wood for a spacer. The rows must overlap evenly.

68 When the asphalt strips reach the dormers, mark where to cut away some of the shingle.

69 Use tin snips to cut the shingle.

70 Cut shingles for the dormer roofs and nail them in place.

71 To finish, cut pieces of shingles for the peaks. These help to waterproof the roof.

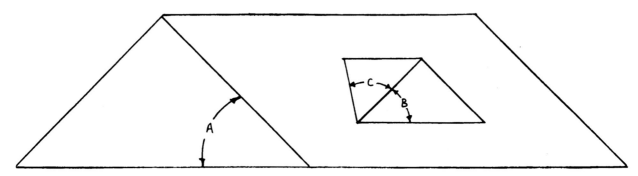

Roof Pitches

Unless you live in a development, it is often difficult to find in a neighborhood two dwellings with identical roof pitches. The same is true with dormers. The Victorian manor sports four dormers, each with a pitch of 45 degrees. The roof pitch of the mansion is also 45 degrees. For the birdhouse builder who wants to be more creative with his roof angles, a table of pitches and cutting angles is provided. The three angles used—and combinations of them—should fit the bill for a variety of styles from Cape Cod to Mansard.

To use the table, decide on the pitch of the roof (A), then the pitch of the dormer (B). C is the angle at which the miter gauge is set. D is the angle for the table saw blade.

Each side or "pitch" of a dormer roof is symmetrical to the other. This means that one cut is going to be a "mirror image" of the other. Be prepared to make some practice cuts on scrap wood first.

Formulas

Here are the formulas used to generate the table of cutting angles. If you are familiar with a scientific calculator, you can experiment with roof and dormer pitches not given in the table. Note: You must calculate the miter angle C first to use in the formula to calculate the saw angle D.

$$C = \tan^{-1}\left(\frac{\sin(B)}{\tan(A)}\right)$$

$$D = \sin^{-1}\left(\frac{\sin(B)\cos(A)}{\sin(C)}\right)$$

Table of Cutting Angles

A	B	C	D
45	45	35	30*
45	30	27	38*
45	60	41	21*
30	45	39*	38*
30	30	41	41
30	60	34*	26*
60	45	22	21*
60	30	16	26*
60	60	27	14*

The table of cutting angles was developed by Stephen Bitel, BA, MA, Adelphi University.

*Note: In the Table of Cutting Angles, some of the angles have stars (*). These indicate that the numbers are the complements of the angles derived from the formulas. For example: If the formula gave 51 degrees, the angle provided in the table is 39 degrees (90 − 51 = 39). These changes are necessary because the table saw blade cannot be set at an angle greater than 45 degrees. If you do experiment with the formulas, determine angles C and D before you make any conversions.

Birdhouse Dimensions

Different dimensions appeal to different birds. While Chuck Grodski uses essentially the same dimensions for most of the birdhouses he makes, you may want to experiment with these suggestions. Keep in mind though, that these are just suggestions. The majority of the birdhouses on Chuck's Long Island property are occupied—and most do not follow a formula.

Species	Floor of cavity (inches)	Depth of cavity (inches)	Entrance above floor (inches)	Diameter of entrance (inches)	Height above ground (feet)
Bluebird	5x5	8	6	$1^1/_2$	5–10
Robin	6x8	8	A		6–15
Chickadee	4x4	8–10	6–8	$1^1/_8$	6–15
Titmouse	4x4	8–10	6–8	$1^1/_4$	6–15
Nuthatch	4x4	8–10	6–8	$1^1/_4$	12–20
House Wren	4x4	6–8	1–6	$1^1/_4$	6–10
Carolina Wren	4x4	6–8	1–6	$1^1/_2$	6–10
Violet Green Swallow	5x5	6	1–5	$1^1/_2$	10–15
Tree Swallow	5x5	6	1–5	$1^1/_2$	10–15
Barn Swallow	6x6	6	B	B	8–12
Purple Martin	6x6	6	1	$2^1/_2$	15–20
Song Sparrow	6x6	6	B	B	1–3
House Finch	6x6	6	4	2	8–12
Starling	6x6	16–18	14–16	2	10–25
Phoebe	6x6	6	A	A	8–12
Crested Flycatcher	6x6	8–10	6–8	2	8–20
Flicker	7x7	16–18	14–16	$2^1/_2$	6–20
Golden-Fronted Woodpecker	6x6	12–15	9–12	2	12–20
Red-Headed Woodpecker	6x6	12–15	9–12	2	12–20
Downy Woodpecker	4x4	8–10	6–8	$1^1/_4$	6–20
Hairy Woodpecker	6x6	12–15	9–12	$1^1/_2$	12–20

A–one or more sides open   B–all sides open

Books by the Experts

JOHN NELSON SCROLL SAW

**50 Easy Weekend
Scroll Saw Projects**
1-56523-108-2
$9.95
By John Nelson
50 patterns for beautiful and
practical projects. Ready to
use patterns.

**Super Simple Clocks
Scroll Saw**
1-56523-111-2
$9.95
By John Nelson
With your scroll saw and quartz
clock movements you can easily
make these 50 examples.

**Advanced Scroll Saw
Clocks**
1-56523-110-4
$9.95
By John Nelson
Five amazing projects never
before published. Complete,
ready to use patterns.

**Scroll Saw
Basketweave Projects**
1-56523-103-1
$9.95
By John Nelson/William Guimond
12 all-new projects for making
authentic looking baskets on your
scroll saw.

**Horse Lovers
Scroll Saw Projects**
1-56523-109-0
$9.95
By John Nelson
A terrific collection of all-new
projects from this popular
author. Ready to use patterns.

**Inspirational Scroll Saw
Projects**
1-56523-112-0
$9.95
By John Nelson
50 plus projects to beautifully
reflect your faith.

WOODCARVING

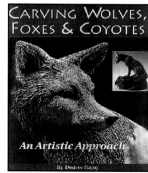

**Carving Wolves, Foxes &
Coyotes:** *An Artistic Approach*
1-56523-098-1
$19.95
By Desiree Hajny
The most complete canine guide in
color. Techniques, reference photos,
anatomy charts, and patterns for
foxes, wolves and coyotes.

Carving Whimsical Birds
1-56523-113-9
$12.95
By Laura Putnam Dunkle
Easy, fun and quick to carve!
Good book for the beginner–uses
commercial turnings.

Folk and Figure Carving
1-56523-105-8
$14.95
By Ross Oar
Explore caricature and realistic
carvings in the 15 projects inside.

MISCELLANEOUS BOOKS

**Making Lawn Ornaments
in Wood ~ 2nd Edition**
1-56523-104-X
$14.95
By Paul Meisel
New edition with 16 pages of
new patterns. Only book on the
subject. Includes 20 ready to use
full-size patterns. Strong seller.

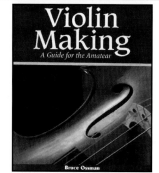

**Violin Making
A Guide for the Amateur**
1-56523-091-4
$14.95
By Bruce Ossman
The easiest book on making
violins in the home workshop.
Complete set of plans included.

**Scrimshaw: A Complete
Illustrated Manual**
1-56523-095-7
$14.95
*By Roger Schroeder &
Steve Paszkiewicz*
Gorgeous full color guide for the
artist and craftsperson. Step-by-
step techniques and patterns.

BOOKS

More Books by the Experts

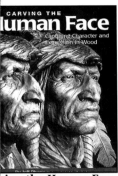

...ving the Human Face
By ...ff Phares
...est book available on
...g faces! A full color guide
...luded.
...ges, 8.5x11", soft cover.
...95 • 1-56523-102-3

Fireplace & Mantel Ideas
By John Lewman
15 ready-to-use patterns and
hundreds of photos showing
installation and design.
90 pages, 8.5x11, soft cover.
$19.95 • 1-56523-106-6

Scroll Saw Relief Projects
By Marilyn Carmin
The first book on fret and relief
work. Includes more than
100 patterns.
120 pages, 8.5x11, soft cover.
$14.95 • 1-56523-107-4

Carving Crazy Kritters
By Gary Batte
Full of creative new designs for
caricature animals. A real winner!
64 pages, 8.5x11, soft cover.
$14.95 • 1-56523-114-7

Creative Christmas Carvings
By Tina Toney
A beautiful and practical full-color
guide to exciting holiday carving
projects.
64 pages, 8.5x11, soft cover.
$14.95 • 1-56523-120-1

...oll Saw Fretwork ...terns ~ Dog Breeds
...udy Gale Roberts
...des dozens of all-new
...gns of "man's best friend".
...ges, 8.5x11, soft cover-spiral
...nd.
...95 • 1-883083-08-7

Scroll Saw Christmas Ornaments
By Tom Zieg
Over 200 ornament patterns, with
brass, copper and plastic designs.
64 pages, 8.5x11, soft cover.
$9.95 • 1-56523-123-6

Scroll Saw Toys and Vehicles Technique & Pattern Manual
By Stan Graves
Create easy, fun toys on your scroll
saw with everyday materials.
56 pages, 8.5x11, soft cover.
$12.95 • 1-56523-115-5

Relief Carving ~ Patterns, Tips & Techniques
By William F. Judt
A complete introduction to relief
carving. Learn tricks of the trade!
120 pages, 8.5x11, soft cover.
$19.95 • 1-56523-124-4

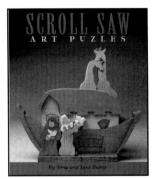

Scroll Saw Art Puzzles
By Tony and June Burns
Includes 32 patterns for cute,
classical and whimsical puzzles.
80 pages, 8.5x11, soft cover.
$14.95 • 1-56523-116-3

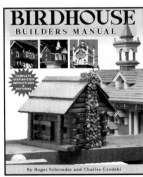

Birdhouse Builders Manual
By Roger Schroeder and
Charles Grodshi
Full patterns, step-by-step photos
and instructions. Sure to please!
120 pages, 8.5x11, soft cover.
$19.95 • 1-56523-100-7

Scroll Saw Workbook
By John Nelson
The best beginner's technique
book from noted author John
Nelson.
96 pages, 8.5x11, soft cover.
$14.95 • 1-56523-117-1

Western Scroll Saw and Inlay Patterns
By Joe Paisley
Exciting new inlay techniques
and lots of new western patterns.
100 pages, 8.5x11, soft cover.
$14.95 • 1-56523-118-X

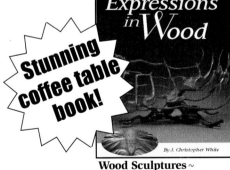

Stunning coffee table book!

Wood Sculptures ~ Expressions In Wood
By J. Christopher White
Stylized carved wooden sculpture
at its best.
128 pages, 9x12, hard cover.
$34.95 • 1-56523-122-8